Conversations
with the
Voiceless

D0815330

Finding God's Love in
Life's Hardest Questions

John Wessells

GRAND RAPIDS, MICHIGAN 49530 USA

Conversations with the Voiceless
Copyright © 2004 by John Wessells

Requests for information should be addressed to:

Zondervan, *Grand Rapids, Michigan 49530*

Library of Congress Cataloging-in-Publication Data

Wessells, John, 1955–
    Conversations with the voiceless : finding God's love in life's hardest questions /
John Wessells.
        p. cm.
      ISBN 0-310-25766-2
    1. Brain damage—Religious aspects—Christianity. I. Title.
RC387.5.W475 2005
617.4'81044'092—dc22

                                                                            2004017336

This edition printed on acid-free paper.

Some names have been changed in this book to protect privacy.

The story of the Day family has been used with permission from Rick, Sally, and Suzanne Day.

The letters by George DelVecchio have been reprinted with permission from Yvonne DelVecchio.

Interior design by Beth Shagene

Printed in the United States of America

---

05 06 07 08 09 10 /❖ DCI/ 10 9 8 7 6 5 4 3 2

To the *voiceless* and their families,
who have spoken volumes into my life

Thank you for inviting me
to be part of your journey

Contents

Acknowledgments

Though this book is written in the first person, it is by no means my work alone. The first person I would like to acknowledge in this joint effort is my wife, Gail. This book would not have been possible had it not been for her love, support, and input. In our early days of courtship, one of the many attractions that drew me to Gail was her willingness and desire to serve our Lord with all her heart no matter what might be asked of her. Her journey has not been an easy one; living by faith, trusting God for every need to be supplied, especially in those early days as we ran together after God's vision for the comatose. Gail, I'm truly in awe of the courage you displayed when asked to endure more than anyone can imagine in the loss of our son. I equate the favor of the Lord in my life purely to you, Gail. "He who finds a wife finds a good thing and obtains favor from the Lord" (Proverbs 18:22 ESV).

Second, I'd like to acknowledge my good friends Scott and Joy Sawyer (whose names really should appear on the front cover of this book, but humbly requested not to). Individually, as writers, you are "masters" of your craft. And to think how blessed I am to have you both share your artistic gifting and abilities together for this one project. Words cannot express my gratitude. But even more important to me is our friendship. Next to my wife and children, your friendship is the greatest gift that I have received from the Lord. You have been a tremendous source of encouragement and love to my family and me for many years. Our many memories together—NYC, Greene, Four Season's, Silo, Tiny Town, Denver, Otego, Rockies, Nuggets, Applebees, oh, and I almost forgot "the kitchen crew"—are priceless!

To my good friends Clyde and Diana Dale, and Roger and Debi Jonker, your love, friendship, and support since the very beginning have encouraged and inspired us to "run the race."

To Don Wilkerson, for guidance and encouragement to pursue the calling. It was your prodding that introduced us to the Sawyers for the *Christianity Today* article. You have been a father in the faith.

To David Wilkerson, for your continued support and encouragement all these years. Brother Dave, thanks for your heartfelt belief in Precious Oil Ministries, Inc. Your timely gifts in our hour of need are greatly appreciated.

To John Sloan, my new friend at Zondervan, for putting legs to this book and believing in its message. Your heart and passion for this project have been a real encouragement. Thank you for showing me "The Barnabas Way."

To the staff at Zondervan, for all your hard work in making this a reality.

To Joni Eareckson Tada, for your life example, encouragement, and insightful understanding into the hearts of the voiceless. Your heartfelt foreword to this book is greatly appreciated.

Portions of this book have appeared in periodicals, in an abridged or other form. I'm grateful to both *Christianity Today* and *The Christian Reader* for publishing these parts of our story.

Most of all, I'm grateful for the opportunity to tell the stories of the head-injured and others of the "voiceless" in our midst. In most cases in this book, their names have been changed to protect their privacy.

Before You Begin

"Why am I living?" Not many people have the guts to ask it out loud, but lots of us think it. There's a slew of self-help books, midday talk shows, and one-hour counseling services to help us find meaning and purpose. Sometimes the purpose is hard to pin down in this quick-fix, fast-paced, no-deposit-no-return culture. Everything's so external. Disposable. Even people for whom there seems no purpose in living.

Case in point: Clay. He was born with his umbilical cord wrapped around his neck, leaving him totally paralyzed and unable to speak, completely deaf and blind. Plus, he needs a ventilator in order to breathe and a feeding tube in order to eat. All this baggage attached to a seventeen-month-old boy. If life's largest questions have answers for him, then there are answers for all of us.

I met Clay at one of our recent Joni and Friends' Family Retreats; his foster parents provide care to him and two other disabled children. After one of our evening sessions, I wheeled up to Clay's mother at the snack shack. She was licking a cone and gently moving Clay's stroller back and forth. I parked next to them and joined the quiet moment of contentment. Looking at her foster son, I asked the obvious question: "How are you able to connect with him?"

His mother tossed the end of the cone. "When Clay cries, I'll gently brush his cheek," she explained, showing me as she lovingly touched his face with the backside of her hand, "and he'll stop right away. This lets me know he's alert."

I leaned over to do the same. As I stroked him, I thought I saw a faint smile. I silently prayed for Clay, asking God to be large in his heart, to speak, "not in words taught us by human wisdom but in words taught by the Spirit, expressing spiritual truths in spiritual words" (1 Corinthians 2:13). I thought of those who would say, "Take out his feeding tube. Let him starve to death. He can't do a thing. His life has no meaning, no purpose."

Second Corinthians 5:16 warns: "Regard no one from a worldly point of view." Elsewhere we are reminded: "So we fix our eyes not on what is seen, but what is unseen."

God's Word is as true for Clay as it is for any one of us. The Spirit expresses truth to him—not in audible words, but spiritual words. Inwardly he is being renewed. His troubles are achieving for him an eternal glory that far outweighs them all. His value is "not on what is seen, but what is unseen." Therefore, we are not to regard him from a worldly point of view. The Spirit is dynamic, kinetic, active, and powerful—and although we can't see the spiritual activity happening in Clay's life, it's there. His is a hidden holiness. We can't measure God's work or quantify it, but it's real. And spiritual activity gives life value, no matter how humble a person's situation.

If Clay's troubles are achieving for him an eternal glory that far outweighs being deaf, blind, and paralyzed, then his reward will be *glorious*. When we stand before Jesus, he may end up achieving greater accolades than any of us. Just think: He is perfectly demonstrating—even if by default—gentleness and self-control, the fruits of the Holy Spirit. He does not complain or lash out. In fact, when he cries, whether due to pain or fear, Clay immediately responds to the smallest of loving touches—the brush of a hand on his cheek.

In so doing, that little boy inspires everyone who takes time to sit next to him and feel his courage. And he's doing it all without lifting a finger, winking an eye, or hearing a word of encouragement. I felt it. I saw it. And I'm the richer for it.

So are my friends, John and Gail Wessells. They minister to people like Clay and his foster mom all the time. And as you read the book you now hold in your hands, your heart will be enriched and blessed too. In *Conversations with the Voiceless*, John shares powerful and poignant stories of people like Clay—and with every story, he peels back the layers of life's meaning, helping us understand what it means to live. Really *live*.

It's my prayer that as you read this special book, you will sense your heart warming to the joy, strength, and power of *being* in Christ. Not doing, but being, "for in him we live and move and have our being" (Acts 17:28). God has his reasons.

He has his purposes. He never does things capriciously or decides with the flip of a coin. The God of the Bible—the Lord who John and Gail uplift with every song, story, and prayer—is an intentional God, brimming over with motive and mission; and his design for those who have no voice might well be to simply live, breathe, and encourage others.

It's enough to put to rest life's hardest questions.

Joni Eareckson Tada
Spring 2004

What *Are* the Normal Questions?

*I*f we're honest, we all have questions. Questions about life, love, money. Happiness, tragedy, death. Questions we seldom voice. Questions about God.

I face these questions on a daily basis, though it may look a little different than what most people face.

What I do is this: I take my twelve-string guitar to head-injury facilities and sing songs and read passages of Scripture to people in comas. I spend my days with people who supposedly can't hear or understand one word I'm singing or saying. (They actually do, but we'll get to that later.)

What I've discovered is that the voiceless, no matter who they are—the comatose, children, the poor, prisoners, the terminally ill, the suffering—have *a lot* to say, as the rest of us sweat and scrape by and live and pray and relentlessly pursue our carefully constructed plans.

Yet what the voiceless have to say doesn't always come in the form of answers. Sometimes it's just the opposite.

What's important is that they're speaking loudly. Shouting, even. Sort of the way I imagine the rocks and hills crying out. And they have a message for us.

One of my first lessons from the voiceless came in my early days of working with the comatose. I was asked to visit a nineteen-year-old boy who was a patient in a head-injury facility some two-and-a-half hours from my home. The boy had been in a terrible car accident and was in a low-level coma. His mother had heard about what I do and asked that I come sing to him.

As I drove the long trip, I wondered what I would say to these hurting people once I got there. I didn't know the boy or his mother. What songs could I sing to reach beyond the boy's injured mind and into the depths of his heart? What message could I give his hurting mom? What could I do for this broken family, as they faced possibly the worst crisis they'd ever known?

I started praying. I'd been in similar situations before.

At that point in my work, I was able to recount story after story of the incredible ways people's lives had been changed. How I'd watched a comatose man tap his foot in perfect time to the song I was playing. How I'd spent time with a young man who later told me he'd become a Christian while in his coma—who had heard every word I'd sung and said to him.

Now as I walked into the head-injury center to meet this boy's mother, I was struck by how "together" she looked. A middle-aged woman, she was classy and nicely dressed. She graciously extended her hand to greet me, and we talked for a few minutes. I could tell she was grateful I'd come.

Finally, she led me into her son's room. I expected to do what I always did—pray, read, sing. I turned my focus on him and began unpacking my guitar.

Before I could start playing, however, the mother started talking again. Her words quickly turned to sobs. For several minutes, she just sat there with her face in her hands, crying.

When she finally raised her head, she began to pour out her heart. She asked question after question, trying to make sense of what had happened:

How could this have happened to my son? He was so alive. He had so much to live for. Look at him, he was such a beautiful boy. Now he's been robbed of life. And I feel like my life has been robbed from me. I don't know how to go on. Where does it end for me? How will it end for my boy?

I could only sit and listen as this crying, trembling, well-dressed mother agonized over her son's tragedy. Everything she had worked, lived, and sacrificed for had been shattered in an instant. And now, as I sat listening, she was slowly coming to grips with the fact that nothing would ever be the same. All she was left with were questions—nagging, unanswerable questions.

She continued to pour out her heart with sob after sob. It went on that way for an hour and a half. At one point, I peeked at my watch. I realized I only had so much time left to offer her words of comfort. And only so much time to work with her son. As she kept talking, weeping, agonizing, and questioning, I felt the opportunity slipping away. I hadn't even had a chance to mention God.

Finally, I realized I didn't have time to do anything for her at all. About that time, the mother finished crying. She also seemed finished talking. She wiped her eyes and thanked me. Just for being there, she said. It made a difference just to have someone to talk to.

I left the room, carrying my guitar case—and I was totally confused. *Why had I just driven two-and-a-half hours to be here?* I wondered. I had wanted to offer Christ's comfort to this woman and to her incapacitated son. I wanted peace to flood the room as I sang, the way it had with so many other patients. I wanted this grieving mother to experience the love that God had for her.

Anybody could have done what I just did, I thought. I was nothing but a warm body, a set of ears, a blank wall for words to bounce off of.

Then, slowly, it dawned on me: That's exactly what I'd been sent for. Questions.

Questions.

And I felt ashamed. I'd sat there tapping my foot while this woman was asking important questions. I'd been preoccupied with my ministry—the work of God, those things I'd been gifted and trained to do. Worship. Pray. Read Scriptures. Offer a few brief answers, if only through a momentary encounter with God.

The problem was, I hadn't yet learned to love the questions. Or to keep asking them. That would come later.

So what are the questions?

In my work—and, I believe, in our lives—the questions always begin the same way. It doesn't matter what our race or age or religion is. The questions arise when we try to make sense out of suffering. When we try to figure out the reasons behind tragedy, pain, deformity, famine, injustice, some aberration in the universe. Especially when that suffering visits us.

In my work, the questions begin when we see someone trapped in a body or mind that doesn't work the way it once did. "What sense does this make?" we ask. "What possible purpose does it serve for somebody who once had so much potential to . . . *exist* this way?"

We look for answers to these baffling, frustrating questions. Because, to us, the only way the situation can ever make sense is if they can be whole again. Healed.

The truth is, we think *answers* are the only way we'll ever feel better about the messiness of our circumstance. The mystery of it. The *unanswerableness* of it. Only an answer—a visible, knowable purpose—will take away the pain.

Our pain.

What would the voiceless say to us if they could speak?

I've had the incredible privilege of hearing from some of those voiceless people. And what they have to say is disturbing. Counter-cultural. Counter-Christian-cultural, even. Because the voiceless speak for God. And their words are untidy, inconvenient, impractical.

And, above all, a huge relief.

Just the way Jesus' words are.

If you're tired—tired, especially, of what you think of as "the Christian way"—I want to invite you to come along with me for what I hope will be a different kind of journey.

God Isn't Tidy

1

The first thing anyone learns in conversation with the voiceless is that God isn't tidy. He's not predictable. Just when you expect him to do one thing, he does another.

I've seen him explode through my carefully built theologies like a Jack-in-the-box. When we truly give ourselves over to the disruptive love of Christ, all our neat, orderly categories are suddenly at risk. Including some of the ways we think about God.

This much became clear to me in the route that led me to work with the comatose. Before then, I was a worship leader in a midsize church. It was a part-time job, and my wife, Gail, worked part-time as well. We wanted it that way, so we could be free to do other ministry work in our spare time—speaking and singing in churches, prisons, and coffeehouses.

Eventually, though, Gail and I both got burned out from all the Christian work we were doing. We felt as if we were on a spiritual treadmill, fulfilling "status quo" ministry in a lot of the places where we spoke or sang. There seemed to be so many religious fads, so much hype. So many "shoulds" and "how-tos." We both found ourselves hungry for something more, something deeper in our faith lives.

Finally, we cast ourselves into the unknown. We prayed for new direction, new hearts. We prayed for God to speak to us.

All that came to me was the term "music therapist."

Suffice it to say, a few months later, we were penniless. We left our brand-new, custom-built home in upstate New York for a cheap travel trailer in rural Pennsylvania—and we began singing to people in comas.

I don't recommend this route for everybody. But it was the right road for us at the time because of what we were learning about life and love and God. The long and short of it is, it was a journey that required what our "status quo" existence hadn't required: *faith.*

Of course, working with the comatose in itself is an act of faith. Sometimes not even an eye-blink or a flicker of recognition will cross the face of someone we're ministering to. All we can do is be truly present with these people, lift up our hearts in song alongside them, speak whatever words of comfort or hope we can.

In the beginning, I *truly* did this work by faith—faith that, somehow, this was part of what Jesus meant by reaching out to "the least of these." Faith that the comatose are among the poor, the imprisoned, the needy—the ones we're called to reach with love.

That's about all I had to go on, because I never really saw much in the way of responses. At least, I didn't think so at the time. Occasionally, a patient's muscles would relax while I sang. But that was about it.

So eventually, I created my own tidy categories for God. I had learned not to expect much.

"I'm not out for results," I'd say. "I'm just here because Jesus wants me here."

But sometimes, in my periods of doubt, I wondered if this ministry was all just a waste of time—God's time. After all, I could have been down in Times Square, helping feed the homeless, the way Gail and I used to do.

In those early days, I was discouraged a lot.

Then there was Rob.

I had been visiting the young man who was Rob's roommate. The young man's parents had invited me to sing to their son, and after a few weeks of visiting him, Rob was moved into the room.

At that time, Rob was one of the roughest cases I had ever seen. He looked as if he might not even be alive. He never moved, apart from his breathing, and his eyes remained closed. Throughout the following weeks, I knew him only as a motionless body across the room.

The only things I knew about Rob came from the chart at the foot of his bed: His name was Rob and he was in a low-level coma (meaning, he showed no response to outer stimuli). The only other background I had on him was from a nurse. She'd told me Rob had been in a car accident in 1988. Since that time, he hadn't shown any signs that he was ever going to emerge from his condition.

One day, when I was singing to Rob's roommate, I decided to move my chair across the room and talk to Rob.

I felt the strongest urge that I should speak to him about bitterness.

At first I thought I might be cracking up. I mean, I knew absolutely nothing about this guy. But I paid attention to the nudge. I pushed my chair over to Rob's bed and tried desperately to remember any passages from Scripture about bitterness.

"Hi, Rob," I said. "I'm John. I'm sure you've been hearing me with your roommate all these weeks. I thought it was about time I introduced myself."

Rob lay still as ever.

"Rob, I feel the Lord wants me to tell you something," I continued. "He wants to tell you not to hang onto any bitterness in your heart. I don't know what that might be, but he does. And whatever it is, it's destroying you inside."

As I spoke, Rob's body visibly tensed up. It was the only movement I'd ever seen him make.

I continued, "God's Word says, 'Create in me a pure heart, O God, and renew a steadfast spirit within me.' God wants that for you, Rob. He wants to clean out all that bitterness from your heart and fill you with his Spirit."

I began singing: "Create in me a clean heart, O God. And renew a right spirit within me."

Within moments, Rob seemed to fill up with anger. Soon he was straining against the manacles that ordinarily kept his wrists from curling. The sight was astonishing. Nobody had seen this guy move at all in the months he'd been here.

I closed my eyes and kept singing.

"Rob, there's only one person who can help you with your heart," I said. "It's Jesus. The doctors might be able to do something to help you recover your body. But only God can bring true life to your heart. And he wants you to know that he sent his son to take on your sins himself and to cleanse you from all sin—if you'll give your heart to him."

I opened my eyes.

Rob's body was now as tight as a piano string. His jaw muscles bulged from intensity as he clenched his teeth. In a moment's time, he began making faces and noises.

I got scared as I saw this happening. I closed my eyes again and just kept singing.

Rob continued to thrash for some five minutes. All that time I silently prayed for him. Then, suddenly, almost as soon as he'd tensed up, Rob fell back in his bed. As I looked closer, a wave of peace seemed to envelop him. I watched as his expression gradually became serene.

A few minutes later, a nurse walked in.

"Wow," she remarked, setting down a tray. "What did you do to him? He's never looked like this before."

I wasn't sure I'd "done" anything to him. But it looked like something important had happened in Rob's heart.

Over the next few weeks, I continued talking to Rob about the love of Jesus. Yet I did it all by faith. I didn't see any further signs that he had understood me at all, but he continued to look peaceful.

A few months later, I didn't know what to expect the day I took my friend Mike along with me to the Milford Head Trauma Center. Mike had come from New York City to visit Gail and me that weekend in our little trailer in Pennsylvania, so he could go with me to the head-injury hospital. Mike was a good harmonica player, and he had brought along his instrument to accompany me on guitar.

It was great to have some company along because going to the hospitals was pretty lonely. Yet, the ironic thing was, every time I took someone new along, it only increased my doubts about this strange ministry of mine. I couldn't help wondering: *Will Mike understand what I'm doing? What if nothing happens today? Will he think I'm making all of this up? Am I really not getting through to these patients?*

As we neared the hospital in Milford, I tried to summon some hope. *Maybe something is happening after all,* I told myself.

Then I remembered Rob and decided we'd go see him first.

I was banking on my earlier experience with Rob as we neared his hospital room. I was trying hard to believe that nothing I'd done with this young guy each week had been in vain.

I began my usual banter.

"Rob, I'd like you to meet a friend of mine," I said, unpacking my guitar case. "This is Mike."

Mike, not knowing the extent of Rob's condition, reached out his hand toward the listless body.

Suddenly, without missing a beat, a trembling hand rose up and came across the bed to shake hands.

I was stunned.

Rob can hear. He's responding. He's actually reaching out to shake hands!

Mike didn't know any differently. He took Rob's hand and shook it.

"Hi, Rob," he said. "How ya doing?"

I sat speechless. Mike started singing a chorus and then blowing on his harmonica. Dumbfounded, I slowly joined him on guitar, still unable to believe my eyes.

The sight of that pale, trembling hand was a sign—a sign that he might be hearing me.

A short time later, I learned something else about Rob. A nurse told me that just before his accident, he had been in a terrible fight with his mother.

Suddenly, I understood more about why I had been prompted to talk to him about bitterness.

One day at the hospital, before I'd started my afternoon rounds with patients, I ran into Rob's physical therapist in the elevator at the hospital. When she saw me, she smiled.

"Did you hear the good news about Rob?" she asked.

"No," I said, eager to hear what she had to say.

"He's come out of his coma. He can answer yes and no questions."

I was thrilled. I couldn't wait to start asking Rob questions.

That day, I plied Rob with every question I could think of. He would answer with a nod or a shake of the head. I even threw in a few trick questions, to make sure he wasn't just nodding and shaking. Sure enough, Rob was tracking right along with me.

He even showed a sense of humor in some of his responses. He'd often give me the opposite answer I was expecting. After that, there were many afternoons I just spent time laughing with Rob.

I also spent many afternoons trying to teach Rob some songs. Of course, he couldn't speak—yet he did mouth the words as I sang the choruses over and over.

One day as we were "singing" together, a nurse walked in. Rob and I had started in on the chorus, "Praise the Name of Jesus."

The nurse just stood there as I sang and Rob mouthed the words. She seemed puzzled.

"But—he can't say anything," she pointed out to me.

I couldn't help myself. I burst out laughing.

"I know," I answered between breaths. "He's singing!"

Maybe it was my imagination, but Rob almost seemed to grin. I think he got a kick out of it too. Over time—and with help—he began to sit upright. Soon he could almost feed himself. Then one day, Rob surprised me again.

I was praying for him, asking Christ to touch his heart every day. When I finished, I looked up and saw Rob as he uttered, "Amen."

That was the first word anyone had heard him speak.

After that, Rob began to talk, albeit very haltingly and slowly. One of the first things he said clearly was "ice cream." I got a kick out of that one.

For a while, there was only one other clear word from Rob: "home." He wanted to go home.

Finally, the day came when I decided I had to ask Rob what I'd been wondering all along.

"Rob, I have to ask you something," I began. "Do you remember when I first came into your hospital room? Remember when I was always singing to your roommate about Jesus?"

Rob nodded.

"You do remember that? Tell me—could you hear what I was saying then?"

He nodded again.

Now came the question I was really curious about. "When I prayed with you that day—did you ask Jesus into your heart?"

Another nod.

I stopped for a moment. "You're sure, Rob? You're not pulling my leg, are you?"

Rob shook his head.

"Good," I said. I couldn't believe this. But then again, I guess I could. "Is the Holy Spirit ministering to you every day now?"

Again, a nod.

After that, I was convinced Rob had heard everything I'd said while in his room, even when he was at his lowest level. And I was convinced he had encountered the love of God in a real way, whenever it had happened.

I was the first person to take Rob outside the hospital after his accident. It was just a short stroll around the block as I pushed him along in his wheelchair. But that was one fantastic block.

I bet Rob had often wondered if he would ever be able to communicate to anyone again. And I thanked God for *both* our sakes that he had helped us to communicate. Because, at that point in my work, I was the one who had needed to be spoken to. I had desperately needed to hear what Rob had to say. I'd needed my tidy world disrupted. I'd needed words of encouragement—*from the voiceless.*

"You keep working hard in your therapy, Rob," I kept telling him. "Try to keep from putting up a stink, okay? That way I can get you in my van and take you home for the weekend. You can go to church with us."

Rob always nodded at that.

We walked by an ice-cream parlor. I remembered one of his first words: *ice cream.* Then I remembered that one of the nurses had told me Rob had been a cook in a restaurant before his accident.

"Rob, I want you to promise me something."

Rob was listening.

"I want you to promise that when you get out of this wheelchair, you'll cook me the best meal you've ever made."

He nodded again. I loved that nod.

Some people might say I was getting Rob's hopes up. But I truly want that meal from him. I don't know if it will happen in the Milford Head Trauma Center—or around another dinner table one day in heaven.

But what I do believe is that Rob wants to cook me that meal ten times more than I want to eat it.

The first lesson of the voiceless: *Real life is always untidy— and full of surprises.*

Kind of like God.

Cheesecake and Chocolate Syrup: *Not* Living by the Rules

2

A lot of us are run by rules. And not necessarily in a good way.

We often have a tidy framework for how life should work. If we just send our kids to the right schools, invest in the right stocks, and live in the right neighborhoods, then we're guaranteed a nice, neat existence.

In my work, sometimes the most rigid people in the hospital room aren't those whose bodies are permanently stiff and distorted. They're those who are sitting right next to the patients. Family members, friends, even ministers learn to cope with tragedy by finding some sort of code or grid that works for them. And most often, they're not even aware of it.

For some, coping means staying busy. They're constantly on the move, caretaking, looking for new hope, or locating the next doctor. They can't stop, even for a minute, because they think they can't afford to. The sad thing is, they're in desperate need themselves—just as much need as the patient they love and are caring for.

There are other traps too. And some of these a lot more subtle. Sometimes we get rigid in our thinking about God and the way he works. We think things need to happen a certain way and become convinced that everything depends on *us.* We somehow believe that we'll be more successful if we just work harder, plan farther ahead, budget better, pray longer.

It can be such a tiring trap—especially if we're working with people where the needs are constant and pressing.

This could have easily happened to me early on in working with the comatose. I was often tempted to believe I needed to do it all—that it all depended on my efforts, my plans. I'd heard lots of advice on how to get the word out, how to organize and strategize. I could have told you all the ways, all the means, all the *rules* that apply to ministry work of this kind.

Thankfully, that didn't happen.

Instead, there was the cheesecake incident.

One weekend Gail and I had a friend come visit us from New York City. Over pizza one night, we told him what was happening in the hospitals. After dinner, we all decided to go out for dessert.

"They've got great rice pudding at the Milford Diner," Gail suggested. "They put a little cinnamon on top of the whipped cream. It's fantastic."

"I don't know about you guys," I said, "but I've got an incredible craving for cheesecake with chocolate syrup."

Gail raised her eyebrows. "Since when have you ever wanted cheesecake with chocolate syrup?" She's the chef in our home and knows what I like. Cheesecake isn't even in the top one hundred.

"I don't know," I said. "All I know is, that's what I want. Let's go."

When we pulled into the parking lot of the Milford Diner, it was fairly deserted. But then, it was late. As we walked in, we were seated by a waitress whom I hadn't remembered seeing before. She was a bit older, probably in her sixties. Her name tag read "Jane."

"How are y'all this evening?" Jane asked. She oozed warmth.

"We're doing great, thanks," Gail said.

"Good," Jane smiled, her pencil poised to write down our order. "What can I bring you?"

"These two want rice pudding," I pointed out to Jane. "But not for me."

"Oh, well then," Jane grinned, "how 'bout I bring you some cheesecake with some good ol' chocolate syrup on top?"

The three of us sat there wide-eyed. Then we burst out laughing. I jokingly said, somewhat under my breath, "I'll take that as a word from God."

The waitress stepped back for a moment. "Are you all Christians?"

"Yes, we are," Gail answered.

"Me too!" Jane said.

That began a lively conversation that continued sporadically between Jane's service to the few other customers in the diner.

At one point Gail asked, "You don't sound like you're from around here, Jane."

"Oh, child, call me Mama Jane," she chirped. "And I'm not from around here. I'm from Indiana."

"How did you end up in Milford, Pennsylvania?"

Jane's expression drooped a bit, but she never lost her smile. "My son, Keith, was in an accident," she said. "He's been in the head trauma center here in Milford."

I quickly glanced at Gail, and our eyes locked. My heart began pounding.

"Keith's been in a coma for almost a year. I've been praying to meet some Christians who could go and pray for him in the hospital," Jane continued. "Maybe—maybe sometime you could go with me and pray for Keith?"

I was simply blown away.

Now it was our turn to tell Jane why *we* were in Milford. We'd sold our home and moved there, not even knowing why at the time. Then we'd discovered Milford had a head trauma center there. I'd been singing there ever since.

Jane began to cry. "I can't believe it," she said.

She began telling us her story. Jane was widowed and had moved to Milford from Indiana just to try to help her son. Now she was working at the Milford Diner every day to pay for her rented room, so she could visit Keith. I got the feeling she would have stayed in the hospital room with him around the clock, if she could.

Lately, she said, Keith had had a chest cold. It was hard for him when his body shook during a cough. It was getting worse every day, and that was complicating his condition.

"Listen, Jane," I said, "how about if I meet you at the hospital on Monday?"

"Oh, that would be wonderful," Jane beamed. "But, you know, Keith isn't in the hospital here anymore."

"Where is he?"

"He's in another hospital, in Cortland, New York. He just got transferred there."

I didn't even know about *that* hospital. "You mean, there's *another* head-injury hospital around here?"

"Sure. It's about two-and-a-half hours from here. And it's much bigger than the hospital here in Milford. Maybe you could sing to some of the people up there, John."

She took the words right out of my mouth.

Because of my schedule at Milford and various other delays, Gail and I weren't able to make it to Cortland for another week or so. She decided to accompany me on this trip, for a couple of reasons. First, we'd been so touched by Jane that night in the diner, we both wanted to meet Keith and sing to him. And second, we both wanted to see this other head-injury hospital. *Were all these centers the same?* we wondered. And would we ever have a chance of getting into another one?

When we finally drove up to Highgate, the head-injury center in Cortland, it was just as Jane had said. Highgate was a lot bigger than Milford hospital. In fact, it was the size of a large hospital in any medium-size town.

It was a Monday, and we expected to find Jane signed in at the front desk, but she hadn't come in yet. Gail and I already had her written permission to visit Keith. So we signed our names and walked to Keith's room on the first floor.

Highgate was much brighter and airier than the center in Milford. Still, the halls had an ominous feel. It was as if the cheeriness was designed to artificially perk up the people who spent their waking hours there, whether patients or families. And underneath it all was that familiar refrain, *no hope, no hope . . .* My first thought was, *I'd better get used to this.*

Then I thought, *No, this isn't something anyone should ever get used to. If I do, then I'll know I'm in trouble.*

We knocked gently on Keith's door before entering. As we stepped inside, there was Keith in bed, lying motionless. He looked like probably a mid-level case. He had brown hair and brown eyes that registered our presence without looking at us directly. And he could move his head and limbs slightly. He looked really drained from the chest cold. But his face looked innocent, like a child's.

"Hi, Keith," I said. "I'm John, and this is Gail. We're friends of your mother. She said we could come to visit you."

Gail leaned over the bed and told Keith a little bit about us. Keith looked even weaker up close. He seemed a bit wary at having these strangers in his room. Even so, we just kept talking to him.

"Keith," Gail said, "we'd like to pray for you. We know it's been hard for you here. God cares for you, and he's with you here—even in these circumstances. Would you let us pray for you?"

Keith craned his head toward us a bit. We couldn't tell what that meant, but he seemed to be slightly more at ease.

So we prayed. As we asked God to bring healing to Keith, I took out a small vial of oil and dabbed some of it on his forehead, anointing him.

Now Keith moved his head toward us a bit more. His face still had the same innocent expression.

At that moment, we heard the door open behind us. It was Jane.

"Hi, Jane," Gail said in a hushed tone. "We were just praying for Keith."

"Yes," I added, "I hope you don't mind. We felt like we should anoint him with oil."

Jane stopped in her tracks. She put her hands to her cheeks and began to weep. "I've been praying for a year that someone would come and anoint Keith with oil," she said. "I've wanted healing for him so badly."

We spent an hour or so with Jane at the hospital that day. She wept even more and poured out her heart to us about Keith's situation. It was heartrending. Often when she came into his room, a nurse or attendant would be handling Keith as if he were nothing more than a slab of meat.

"I want you to come back, " she cried. "I'm going to talk to these people and see if you can't come in here and sing to *all* the patients."

About two weeks later, Gail and I went back to the Milford Diner. As we'd hoped, Jane was there, across the restaurant. We waved, and when she saw us, she rushed over. She was beaming.

"Hi, children," she said in her warm drawl, grabbing us each by the hand. "I have to tell you all about Keith." She led us to a table and sat us down.

"Ever since you prayed for my son, all the nurses can talk about is how fast he's improved," she said. "His chest is all cleared up."

"Jane, that's wonderful," I said.

"Not only that," Jane said, refusing to be interrupted, "I talked to Keith's caseworker, and she said you can come visit Keith anytime you want."

"Really?"

"Yes," she beamed, her hands quivering with joy while holding ours. "All she asks is that you stop in and see her at the hospital the next time you go there."

The next time was the following week. I was anxious to visit with Keith again. And I was just as anxious to see his caseworker. I wanted to know for sure if we'd been miraculously granted access to Keith, and that it wasn't just wishful thinking on Jane's part.

"Hi, I'm John Wessells," I said as I introduced myself to the friendly looking woman in the caseworker's office.

"Hello, John. I know all about what you do from Jane," she said immediately.

I gulped. I hoped what I did was all right with the hospital.

"I want you to know that you have free access to Keith while you're here . . ."

Good. Jane was right after all.

". . . which brings up another question I have for you."

Uh-oh. Here it comes.

"Would you be interested in working with other patients here?"

The caseworker had no idea what ran through my head when she asked me that question. It was of the image of a small slice of cheesecake with chocolate syrup dripping down the sides.

"Yes, I would," I said. "I'd be very interested."

So much for well-planned-ministry strategies. God was obviously breaking all the rules.

We're all under so much pressure. Everywhere you look, people are burning out, suffocating under the burden of working sixty-hour weeks, topping sales figures, running multiple committees, dieting down to a size six.

And, can I say it? Attending too many church meetings. Reading too many books on how to have perfect families. Listening to too many seminar speakers who tell us how to run successful ministries.

Maybe we should be listening to the voiceless instead. What I think they're saying is this: Truly, as Christ told us long ago, the yoke is easy and the burden is light. It really is. *Let go.*

A guy like Keith has no other options. He can't read the Bible. He can't even open it. In fact, he may not even be able to consciously pray.

All he can do is *be.* And that's okay.

Because God loves him. And God *wants* to show his love to him.

That's why the same loving God will allow a stranger's stomach to growl for a piece of cheesecake, at just the right moment.

We just gotta stop being so darn religious.

Is Life a Sweet,
Neat Package?

3

Our hearts are designed with built-in emotional filters. And those filters have an important function. They're designed to help screen out some of the unpleasantness around us. On one level, these heart-filters are gifts; they help us to navigate and make sense of a broken world. Yet, on another level, our filters can be our souls' own worst enemies.

Here's a simple question: What do we do when someone in our family has the TV turned up too loud? Easy; we pick up the remote and turn down the volume. We simply take control of the annoyance. Most of us do the same thing when the evening news is filled with downer reports and images. We pick up the remote and change the channel. We can't stand the agitation it brings to us. Who in his right mind doesn't take control of his surroundings this way?

We tend to have the same approach to life. When life throws a screeching, painful situation at us, our first reaction is to want to turn down the volume. We reach for some invisible remote control in our hearts to try to change the channel. Nobody wants to be confronted with the miseries this world can hurl at us. And who can blame us? Society doesn't. From

TV to self-help books to medicine to advancements in technology, we're urged to maximize our happiness and minimize our pain.

But what happens when our resources don't work? How do we react, for example, when we can't turn down the volume of a spouse's chronic physical pain? What do we do when we can't make things better for our aging parent, our sick child, our suffering friend?

We don't want the hard questions. We want our lives to fit in a neat package. A sweet, neat package of answers.

I want to tell you the true stories of two women. You've probably read about them at one time or another. Both of them once led vibrant lives with promising futures. But they suffered serious, perhaps irreversible head injuries that altered their lives forever. At the time I first met them, I couldn't imagine what their parents were going through. I couldn't imagine what it was like to face the decisions they faced.

But I do know that, in different ways, these voiceless women spoke to me. Loud and clear.

On a gray, windy February day, I steered the car into the parking lot of the Missouri Rehabilitation Center in Mount Vernon. I realized I hardly recognized the place—even though I'd been there only two months before. *Where are all the protesters carrying signs?* I thought in reflex. *Where are all the media and the police?*

That past December, Gail and I had come to the center from upstate New York. We had wanted to try to visit two comatose girls. One of them had had her feeding tube removed. She was legally being starved to death.

Now, surveying the quiet grounds of this hospital, I thought of the improbable chaos of that previous visit: television crews, pro-life protesters, state troopers, beefed-up security. On the surface, at least, everyone had come to the hospital on behalf of the starving girl.

Everyone had come with answers.

Less than a year before, Gail and I knew nothing of the Missouri Rehabilitation Center. And very little about the issues surrounding euthanasia. For three years we had spent our days visiting comatose patients in head-trauma centers—offering prayer, reading Scripture, singing songs, holding Bible studies for patients and their families. All we knew was that God loved these people, and he wanted to reach out to them in their pain and questioning.

One afternoon I picked up an issue of *Time* magazine. The cover photo grabbed my attention immediately: a disfigured young woman lay comatose in a hospital bed. A feeding tube protruded from her stomach. Her father sat forlornly at her side. The headline on the cover read in stark letters: "The Right to Die."

The picture startled me. This girl looked like the kind of people I sang to every day. On the other hand, she looked as if she were on a much higher functioning level than most of my patients. Many of them lay in low-level comas, showing little or no physical response to stimulus.

This girl's name was Christine Busalacchi. Something immediately told me that Gail and I would be meeting her. I dove into the cover story, which mentioned her father's legal battle to have Christine's feeding tube removed. It also mentioned that she and another comatose girl, Nancy Cruzan, were in the same rehabilitation center somewhere in Missouri.

As it happened, Gail and I had been invited to speak the following spring at several churches in the Midwest, including Missouri. I knew we had to make a trip to that hospital.

As the weeks passed, we felt an increasing desire to get to Missouri, so we rescheduled our spring trip for mid-December. On December 12 we packed our van full (including our six-month-old son, John Samuel) and drove west. Little did we know that just two days later, in Indiana, we would read that the courts had ruled to allow Nancy Cruzan's parents to remove her feeding tube.

The following day's newspaper brought more news from the head-injury center in Missouri. People from all over the country were converging on the center to protest the court's ruling.

On December 17, we finally arrived in Mountain Grove, Missouri, at the home of our close friends, Clyde and Diana Dale. The Dales lived only an hour and a half from the hospital in Mount Vernon. As soon as our bags were unpacked, Clyde showed me that morning's newspaper. It was filled with accounts of the protest, which was growing larger by the day. Pictures showed protesters and police surrounding the hospital. Now I wondered if we would ever see Nancy or Christine at all. Then I noticed a quote in the newspaper by a chaplain from the hospital; I wrote down his name as a possible contact.

The next morning we all decided that only the Dales' adult son, Martin, and I should make the drive to Mount Vernon. We thought it wise to check out the scene at the hospital because of the news accounts. Yet, as Martin and I pulled up to the Missouri Rehabilitation Center, I realized nothing could have prepared me for what I saw.

Helicopters circled overhead. Television crews lit up the grounds. Police stood blocking the hospital's entrances. And protesters swarmed everywhere. They had set up a tent village. And they were marching in front of the hospital, holding up signs and placards. The whole scene was a mass of confusion.

Martin and I parked the van and made our way through the crowds to the hospital's front entrance. We were greeted by a half-dozen state troopers. I asked if we could talk to the chaplain. The officers examined us, then looked at one another, stepped aside, and opened the door. We walked inside and quickly were pulled aside by an officer. Another trooper went to get the chaplain for us.

A few moments later, the head chaplain walked up to us. His name was Ted Coleman. I introduced myself and gave him a brochure describing what we do.

"This is what we're about," I explained. "I feel strongly that God wants us to spend some time with Nancy Cruzan and Christine Busalacchi."

The chaplain laughed under his breath and shook his head. "You're about the three-hundredth person here today who's been sent by God," he said. He then began reeling off some disturbing stories about the bizarre characters who'd shown up as God's emissaries.

After the third story, I held up my hand, somewhat apologetically. "I can see why you're hesitant," I said. "But we're not here for the media hype or any issue. We only came here to share the love of Christ through music with these two women."

At that, his look softened. I knew he could see that we'd traveled all this way to do just that. He stood thinking for a moment.

"I'm the only one who has contact with the Cruzans," he said. "I'll give them your brochure and tell them you're here. But I'll have to get back to you."

Before Ted could leave, a flash of hot lights burst on all around us. A procession of wheelchair-bound people had appeared in the hallway. They all looked like head-injury patients. And they were being wheeled out the hospital doors by police officers.

"What's going on?" I asked Ted.

"Those are the rescuers," he said. "They tried to get in to see Nancy. They've refused to leave, so the authorities are carrying them out."

One by one, these people were wheeled outside and promptly dumped on the front steps. But they didn't get up. Instead, they sat praying in loud voices. In a flash, TV cameras hovered over them, zooming in on their faces. It was a circus.

Ted told me this wasn't the half of it. Some protesters had brought in a nurse with a feeding tube to try to slip into Nancy's room and resume feeding her. Then a man carrying a glass of water had shown up. He said someone inside was thirsty and he needed to give her a drink, because the Scriptures commanded him to.

My heart sank. I hadn't been prepared for any of this. I thought I'd come to Missouri to sing to a dying girl and tell her about Jesus. But obviously that wasn't going to happen. It all seemed tragically ironic: I'd never had any trouble getting in to see head-injury patients before, because no one else ever bothered to visit them. But now, because believers had banded together to "fight for life," I might not get a chance to share the love of God with a dying girl. It made me sad.

Then I thought of Christine. I asked Ted about possibly seeing her—but he shook his head. The security restrictions applied to her as well.

There was nothing more we could do. Martin and I thanked the chaplain and drove back home to Mountain Grove. That night our families gathered and prayed for Nancy, as we would every night for the rest of the trip.

I went back the next morning to see if Ted Coleman had given our brochure to the Cruzan family. Ted said he had told the Cruzans about us. But, not surprisingly, they'd simply had it with Christians. At this point, they weren't open to seeing anyone.

I kept coming to the hospital every other day or so, hoping Ted would tell me the Cruzans had changed their minds. But nothing ever changed. I finally saw that all we could do was to continue praying for Nancy—and wait.

During that time, I saw Nancy's father do something that struck me as incredibly kind. When he saw all the protesters outside and how freezing cold it was, he went and bought a coffee pot and an extension cord. He wanted them to at least have a hot cup of coffee to help keep them warm. I've never forgotten that.

❦

Christmas Day arrived and that morning we went with the Dales to help out at a local mission. We had a wonderful time dishing out food, leading worship, and sharing Jesus with people who had no place to go for the holiday. The next morning we all were laughing about an experience at the mission when Martin came in with the morning newspaper. His face was heavy.

"Nancy died this morning," he said.

Everyone was speechless. Suddenly, I realized how strongly I'd believed we would get to see Nancy before she died. But we never made it.

All the way home to New York, Gail and I wondered aloud why we'd gone there. The hospital experience had been so chaotic. We had been dazed by the whole ordeal. When we stopped at a couple of churches where we were scheduled to speak, we couldn't hide our dejection.

Three weeks later, in late January, we still hadn't shaken off our confusion when I received a phone call from someone named Peggy Cooper. She told me she was one of the chaplains of the Missouri Rehabilitation Center. She had learned about us through a brochure we'd given Ted Coleman. She was wondering if we'd be interested in coming back to Missouri. She wanted us to visit Christine.

I couldn't believe my ears. Suddenly, I was flooded with the feelings I'd had when I first saw Christine's picture on the cover of *Time*.

"There's just one catch," Peggy noted. "You have only fourteen days to get here. Christine's father wants to move her to a different hospital. Right now the Rehabilitation Center has legal guardianship over her, but that's only for two more weeks."

Immediately I told Peggy we'd come, and we hung up. Within three days, Gail, John Samuel, and I were in Missouri again, driving with the Dales to the Rehabilitation Center.

This time, the hospital grounds lay so bare it was eerie. There were no tents, no protesters, no media crews. And the doors were wide open, with no state troopers to greet us. Instead, we were met inside by several of the chaplains—Ted Coleman, Peggy Cooper, and George Wilson—each of them grinning.

"We're behind you," Ted told us. "We want you to feel free to do whatever it is you do."

We all squeezed into an elevator and took it to the third floor, where a group of nurses met us. They seemed just as excited to see us as the chaplains had been. Now an entire entourage rambled down the hallway to see—finally—Christine.

The room they led us to could have been that of any other comatose person. Greeting cards, old and new, hung from a bulletin board. Pictures of family and friends stood on a bedstand. A blank TV screen stared down from the facing wall. And lying in bed was an almost motionless figure, facing the window. A nurse called her name—and Christine turned her head and looked at us.

When I first saw her gaze, I couldn't believe this was the same girl as pictured on the cover of *Time.* She looked so alive!

And she was all dressed up instead of left lying in bed with her stomach and feeding tube exposed. She was wearing makeup; her hair was styled. And she was smiling from ear to ear. Every person in the room was struck by the strong sense of life exuding from this girl. She obviously was much higher-functioning than the magazine cover had portrayed.

As we gathered around her bed, Christine saw little John Samuel in my arms. Immediately, her eyes brightened. She exhaled a long wheeze—a laugh! John Sammy cooed back at her, and Christine gave an awkward giggle. She seemed to enjoy it all.

I took my guitar out of the case. Someone began to pray, and I picked out the opening chords of "There Is None Holy as the Lord." As we sang, a peaceful presence filled the room. Christine remained focused in on us—she was absorbing everything. A few moments later, as we sang "As the Deer Panteth for the Water," she was still right alongside us.

We continued worshiping a while, and Christine simply seemed to melt. Her entire body relaxed, as many patients do when Gail and I worship with them. At one point, I stopped and explained to Christine what was going on. I spoke very simply to her about salvation and how Jesus had died for her sins. I told her about forgiveness—that all she had to do was open her heart to Jesus, and she could enjoy new life right where she was. She seemed to understand everything I said.

When we finished our time with Christine, the chaplains told us they fully approved of everything we'd done.

"You've got blanket permission to come in here anytime," Ted said.

The next day we came to the hospital early, eager to spend time with Christine again. We went to her room on our own and began worshiping, just as we had the day before. This time, however, we were interrupted by a supervising nurse.

"I'm sorry," she said. "There's a court order preventing anyone other than chaplains from being in Christine's room."

We were dumbfounded.

"However," she added, "I do believe Christine can participate in group meetings."

"What constitutes a group?" I asked.

"Hmm," she pondered. "Well, I think it takes just one other person." With that, two enthusiastic nurses wheeled Christine and another brain-injured girl, Linda, out of their rooms. They headed toward the end of the hallway. Instantly, we had our group.

The sounds of our worship spread throughout the entire floor. One high-level patient wheeled himself over, then another. Nurses maneuvered wheelchairs holding low-level patients. Soon a small crowd had gathered. Everyone, it seemed, could sense more than just music.

A few moments later, the hospital administrator appeared. I stopped playing my guitar, but he encouraged me to continue. "I don't see anything wrong with what you're doing," he smiled. "Feel free to do it, as long as you do it this way."

Before we left that day, we all turned to say goodbye to Christine. She answered with a long, loud gasp—"Uuuuhhh"— the sound head-injured people often make when they want to speak. We knew it was her "goodbye." Then, unbelievably,

Christine lifted an arm about fifteen inches above the tray on her wheelchair. *It was a wave.*

The next day, as we filed from the elevator onto the third floor, Christine spotted us from some thirty feet away. She saw me carrying my guitar—and instantly she began to smile. "Uuuuhhh," she gasped, and she raised her arm again in a wave. She recognized us.

Every hour we spent at the hospital was full. At one point, the director of activities asked us to visit other head-injured patients on the fourth and fifth floors. We gladly agreed—and on each of those floors, some twenty patients of various levels were wheeled into an activity room. We held special worship services, and many patients wept as we sang. Later, several indicated as best they could that they wanted to know Jesus. Gail and I prayed at length for one distraught girl whose tears streamed nonstop down her cheeks.

One afternoon Gail, the Dales, and I sat with Christine in the hallway. I opened my Bible and read aloud from Isaiah 55:1 (ESV): "Come everyone who thirsts, come to the waters."

I turned to our new friend. "Christine, God says if you're thirsty, you can drink in his Spirit," I said. "Are you thirsty?"

Christine turned to look at me, then opened her mouth. Lifting her arm, she pointed her index finger to her tongue. Then she made a low noise: "Nnnhhh . . ."

We were astonished. "Yes, you're thirsty," I said. "Christine, Jesus' Spirit in you will never run dry."

In our nine days at the hospital, we saw many such people—voiceless yet fully alive—touched by the love of God. Gail and I truly were sad when the day came to go home. Yet we were reassured by the care and concern that the hospital staff had for the patients and, especially, for Christine. Before we left, a nurse promised to keep us updated on her status.

As it turned out, Christine remained at the Missouri Rehabilitation Center for several months. Eventually, however, her father moved her to a hospital in St. Louis. At that point we lost all contact with her.

In the months immediately following, Gail and I heard occasional news reports on court decisions regarding her father's legal battle to remove Christine's feeding tube. For over a year we heard nothing more. Then, one February, we learned that Christine's feeding tube had finally been removed. She was deprived of all food and water.

I was incredulous when I read the *New York Times'* report that the tube "was removed . . . after a team of neurologists at Barnes [Hospital in Saint Louis] confirmed that Miss Busalacchi was in a persistent vegetative state . . . The diagnosis . . . was consistent with diagnoses made by other physicians since Miss Busalacchi was injured [in 1987]. Persistent vegetative state . . . is characterized by the incapacity to speak, think or move voluntarily."

Christine died the next month. Her obituary in the *Times* stated that "the cause of death was cardiac arrest due to dehydration . . . The medical team at Barnes said Miss Busalacchi did not feel pain or suffer as her body dehydrated . . . The team said it was impossible for people in her condition 'to feel thirst, hunger, pain or suffering.'"

Needless to say, the *Times'* coverage of the ordeal, like *Time* magazine's cover photo, didn't reflect our experience with this vibrant young woman. During that week in March when Christine was without food and water, Gail enlisted all our friends to pray for her as she was starving. We couldn't bear to think about her in such agony.

What did these two women say to me?

Here's what I learned from Nancy Cruzan: The hospital chaplains at the Rehabilitation Center told us something very revealing. Despite all the protesters who had once shown concern for her, no one had ever returned to show similar concern for the other forty or more brain-injured patients who remained there after Nancy died.

And it makes me wonder: *Why is it so much easier to care about causes than about people?*

In this case, I'm talking about both sides of the issue. We *all* want a sweet, neat package. On one side, we want to believe the news accounts that those two young women didn't suffer when they were no longer given food. On the other hand, we want to believe that caring means protesting outside hospitals.

I'm not sure I have any answers anymore. I just know that Christine Busalacchi once pointed to her tongue to let me know she was thirsty for the love of God.

That's all I know.

Who Are
the Real Prisoners?

4

I'll be honest: I've had a lot of difficulty over the years raising financial support for our work with the comatose. I mean, who would really want to give toward what we do? Most Christians want to give their money to projects that yield results you can actually *see.* I realized long ago, though, that the only way anyone would want to give to us is if they glimpsed God's heart in what we do.

As time went by, I grew more convinced that these voiceless ones are truly among those whom Jesus mentions in the Sermon on the Mount: "Blessed are the poor in spirit, for theirs is the kingdom of heaven. Blessed are those who mourn, for they shall be comforted" (Matthew 5:3–4). Yet, how could I best convey that need to others?

Like many people I know in ministry, Gail and I struggled with our food and electric bills each month. Sometimes, it was easier to talk to people about the other outreaches we were involved in: feeding the homeless in Times Square, for instance, or singing to the incarcerated in prisons. Most Christians understand that Jesus wants his church to care for the poor and to visit those in prison. And, rightly so, they'll give their time and money to support those kinds of works.

Eventually, though, I discovered that even our financial struggles were accompanied by yet another important—and unexpected—lesson from the voiceless:

What happens when the poor and those in prison decide to care for and visit *you*? Nothing can be more humbling.

In the weeks and months following our visit with Christine, I wanted to let more people know about the needs of the comatose. So, during that time, some friends of ours offered to write a couple of magazine articles about our work. A few months after one of those articles appeared in *Christianity Today*, Gail and I received a surprising letter.

Dear John and Gail,

My name is George Del Vecchio. I am on death row in Illinois. I read about you in Christianity Today *recently. I was moved, touched to hear about what you folks do. I asked my friends in New Hampshire to get your address for me because I felt a strong need to communicate with you. They contacted you and then sent me your address.*

It was Saturday, March 6, when I received the Christianity Today *containing your story. I never thought of such a ministry, never heard of such, and I was amazed at how much I found myself identifying with people in comas. On death row, you tend to be forgotten; your life is on hold while you just wait for death, in most cases. People tend to think we can't be reached, that our lives have no value or meaning, and so we are not worth the effort. We suffer and our families suffer with us. We're just here.*

This prison is located in southern Illinois, so we receive the St. Louis TV stations. I have followed the story of Christine Busalacchi. I was very bothered by what I was hearing. As I read your story, I found myself thinking of her, wondering if she might someday awake as that one fellow did that you ministered to. I wondered if anyone had taken the time to minister to Christine Busalacchi; I was concerned for her as I read your story, because I knew they talked about removing her feeding tube and killing her. I thought of her that Saturday night, cried for her, prayed for her.

The next day, Sunday, March 7, I heard on the news that she had died early that morning. I felt sad, and I felt great anger. You see, one day I was watching the news and they talked about how someone was trying to stop them from killing her, saying it would be cruel and painful for them to starve her to death. I recall they reported one of her doctors saying that, "No, it's not cruel, it won't hurt her—she won't suffer, because she isn't aware of pain and suffering," or words to that effect.

Some say, "Well, how do you know that?" I found myself asking this question: "If she feels no pain, and will not suffer from being starved to death, then why do it?" Her father and the doctors say they want to put an end to her suffering, yet the doctors say she isn't aware. Then why put her out of a suffering she isn't aware of?

Really, whose interest do they have at heart? Are people tired of dealing with her? Or maybe it hurts them to see her this way? If so, is their pain reason to kill her? If she doesn't know pain and suffering, then why not let her live, give God a chance to work a miracle, and wake her up? Give her time to hear the gospel? I had all kinds of questions. One question in the back of my mind was: Did John and Gail Wessells know of Christine and minister to her?

I have no words to describe the joy I felt in my heart when I learned that you had! I thank God for you, and I thank you both from the bottom of my heart. What a precious and wonderful ministry you have. I feel strongly that people should know about and support your work, so I have done what I can to help. I don't have much to give—on death row, we are kept in our cells, not allowed out, so we can't work and earn anything. What little we have is from friends and family who help from time to time. But I want to share what I can. Earlier today, I made out a prison voucher and had ten dollars taken from my account to be sent to you; they are slow, so it may take a week or two to reach you. But it is on its way. When I can, I will send you what I am able. It might only be five or ten bucks at a time, but I want to help you folks minister to those people and their families.

Also, this past week I have written letters telling people about you and encouraging them to pray for you and support you financially. And we are allowed to make collect phone calls, so I have also called a number of people to tell them. And most all of them have asked me for your name and address, and some even wanted your phone number. So I have shared this information with them, and I believe a good number of them will follow through. They come not only from the Chicago area, which is my home, but also from other places around the country. And I have many others yet to contact, which I am doing.

In another life, I was once a very messed-up guy. I did a lot of wrong, sinned a lot, and caused a lot of grief to myself, my family, and to innocent others. I'm 45 years old as of last month. I have spent 23 1/2 of the last 28 years in prison. I have been locked up on this case since 1977, have been on death row since 1979. Before that, I spent from 1965—when I was 16—until 1973, when I was 25, in prison. After my last arrest, people pretty much gave up on me. They thought I was hopeless . . . not worth the effort.

However, God moved on my heart—why, I don't know, other than he loves me despite all the evil I did—and he sent some wonderful people into my life. They witnessed to me, loved me, and reached out to me with the gospel. If not for that, I'm sure I would have killed myself long ago, simply because I was so miserable and could not have survived had not the Lord come into my life. And all through these many years on death row, the Lord has been faithful, sustaining me, changing me, and growing me up in his grace, and he has brought into my life many wonderful Christian people to encourage and support me along the way . . .

God has blessed me greatly, has given me a new mind and heart, has put a new Spirit into my being. I don't know what the future will bring, don't know if I will live and go free, spend my life in prison, or soon be executed. What I do know

*is that Jesus saved me and God blessed me wonderfully, and
whatever he has planned, I trust him. Sure, I hope and pray it
is life and freedom. How wonderful it would be to live a free
life with the Lord. It would be a joy I once never knew to be
possible, and I'd like to experience it. But I trust him no matter
what . . .*

As promised, we received the check for ten dollars just a
few weeks after George first wrote to us. It was the first of several letters and small monetary gifts he sent to us.

Soon we began a regular correspondence. Through those
letters, Gail and I discovered more about George: how he'd
committed his crimes while high on PCD and LSD. The shame
and remorse and guilt he'd felt over what he'd done. How loving people had introduced him to forgiveness and restoration
in Christ.

As George shared more of his story with us, we responded
with some of our own hopes and struggles as well. In his letters, he was always encouraging, always telling us to keep up
the good work.

"Sorry to hear about the financial problems," he wrote in
one. "Thankfully the Lord is giving you some work to tide you
over. One way or the other, he always helps us to make it
through. I can tell you, although my time and experience here
has been difficult in ways I can't rightly describe, one thing for
sure is that he has helped me survive it all. Despite the hard-
ship, today I am a better man than I ever thought possible."

George seemed to relate to and understand what Gail and
I were doing in ways we rarely experienced. And he always

seemed to have great clarity about what was most important in life. He once wrote:

> *I don't know, but maybe it's because of the suffering I have known and caused, the pain and wasted lives involved with my own life—maybe this has something to do with why I see things the way I do these days. But God has put a burden on my heart for how precious life really is. Maybe the innocent blood I shed somehow helped to wash the blindness and stupidity from my own eyes so that I could see reality.*
>
> *For sure I know the blood of Christ washed away my sin, cleansed my soul. I know that as part of teaching me, healing me, and changing me, God himself worked to break my own heart. He put me in touch with the horror and pain of my life, of how my sin has caused so much grief to people. Yes, he broke my heart wide open. I think he had to do that in order to let out the pain, anger, and sin. And then he gave me a new heart that was full of new and wonderful things.*

During the time we were in contact with George, he was in the process of appealing his case. Gail and I were eager to stay current with what was happening in his life. Soon, he started calling us every Sunday night, when prison rules dictated he could talk for exactly 59 minutes. We always used up every single minute.

One evening during our conversation, I suddenly remembered something important: I had some good friends living in his area, just across the river from where the prison was. I told George I'd ask if they could come visit him.

Sure enough, they said they'd be glad to. It wasn't long before members of our friends' church family visited George as well. They also reached out with love and support to George's mother, who also lived in the area.

Then came the day we received the news none of us wanted to hear: George had lost his appeal.

His attorney would continue the process of trying to gain a last-minute stay of execution. But despite that, his date for lethal injection was set for the day before Thanksgiving of that year. And among one of his final requests was to see me before he died.

Twelve days before his execution date, I flew to Illinois to see George, to spend time with him face-to-face. What I remember best about our conversation were the questions: George was struggling with letting go. He didn't want to die, and he didn't know if he should keep fighting. I tried to encourage him the best I could, reminding him that, even if he lost his appeal, he'd soon be in the presence of the Lord.

It was another of those moments in life when I felt completely inadequate for the task. What do you say to a man who is staring death in the face? I did my best to enter fully into his questions and struggles with him.

As we hugged goodbye, we both had tears in our eyes. I think we both knew deep down it would be the first—and last—time we would see each other in this life. I flew home, and within days our friends called us with the news: George's stay of execution had not been granted.

The day George went home to be with Jesus was a sad day for me. But there is something I suspect, something that makes me smile even to this day: I believe that man stumbled upon a very large treasure heaped in heaven, just for him.

Who Are the Real Prisoners?

We all know that Jesus tells us to visit those who are in prison. But nothing prepared me for the day when a prisoner came to visit *me*, with love and support and encouragement. George's letters and the financial gifts, small as they might be, meant everything to Gail and me in our daily lives. They kept us going on many discouraging days.

It also helped me realize that, up to that time, my definition of "prisoner" was pretty narrow.

You see, it's easy to view the prison of a comatose person's body—the rigidity, the slack face, the twisted limbs. And it's not hard to see that those who are incarcerated within four cement walls and cold steel bars are trapped in a similar way.

But a man like George disrupted all my definitions. He helped me realize that, to whatever extent you or I might be shortsighted or self-centered, *we* are in prison.

Here was a man who gave the widow's mite: everything he had went toward the sake of the gospel. And his example encouraged me that I could do the same. It doesn't matter what we have to give—an encouraging letter or a prison voucher for ten dollars. The smallest things matter. A lot. In fact, sometimes they matter *the most.*

Whatever prison we might find ourselves in—financial needs, marital problems, spiritual struggles—we can still give of ourselves for the sake of something higher. We can still give our widow's mite.

Like our friend George, sometimes the voiceless are the ones most fluent in the language of the kingdom of God.

Journeying
with the Voiceless

5

"We walk by faith, not by sight" (2 Corinthians 5:7 ESV). Sometimes this is easier said than done.

Often when I hear this familiar verse, I think of the people mentioned in the book of Hebrews—those who truly took these words to heart: Abraham. Isaac. Jacob. Joseph. Moses. Rahab. Their faith seems so much bigger than mine—and a lot more glamorous.

But then I remember that each of them had to live out their journey of faith the same way we all do—in the midst of the mundane routines of everyday life.

I don't know about you, but sometimes it takes everything in me to have the faith just to keep going. Just to keep putting one foot in front of the other and to leave the rest to God. I'm talking about the faith it takes to engage with daily life: Worrying about paying your bills on time. Trying to be a good husband or a good parent.

You see, we're designed to truly *walk by faith*. Yet, contrary to much opinion, this doesn't usually mean anything glorious. I'm convinced that walking by faith means, for the most part, walking in the everyday, in the ordinary. And sometimes, that's the toughest thing of all to do.

The voiceless know all about that.

It was a brisk morning in December when I drove to the Milford Head Trauma Center. As I stood waiting for the elevator to take me to the second floor, I glanced nonchalantly into an adjacent room. A head-injured young man lay motionless in bed—and for some reason he caught my eye.

He was young—maybe still in his teens—and he was in bad shape.

I had passed by this room many times before. I'd probably even looked in several times, but I had never really noticed him. Today, however, as I glanced at him, something stirred in my heart.

A woman sat near his bed, tending to him and overseeing the nurses' handling of things. She had a mother's protective instincts. She looked assertive and self-assured, as if she knew exactly what should be done for her son. And yet her eyes reflected the desperation I saw in so many family members here at the hospital.

After that day, I felt the same urge each time I came to Milford. As I stood waiting for the elevator, I felt the urge to go spend time with this mother and son.

Four months later, in April, there I was again, standing near the elevator, talking with the director of volunteers. We were scheduling a time for me to see some new patients at the hospital. As we talked, a friendly looking man walked up.

"Excuse me," he asked, "are you the fellow who plays the music?"

"Yes, I am," I said.

A smile spread across his face. Yet, even so, the smile betrayed a hint of desperation.

"I was wondering," he began nervously. "My wife and I would like you to come and play for our son. Would you mind?"

"Not at all," I said. "Who's your son?"

"He's right in there."

The man pointed to the room by the elevator—and I knew right away who his son was.

At last—the guy I'd been waiting for.

As I finished up business with the director of volunteers, I could hardly contain myself. I wondered what was in store for this young man.

When I walked into the room, the father stood by his son's bed. The mother rose from her chair and extended her hand to me.

"Hi, I'm Terri," she said.

"I'm John," I said. "It's nice to meet you."

"I'm Ted," the man said. Both he and Terri looked determined, but in different ways. He seemed to be trying to be upbeat about his son's condition. Terri's determination seemed more about being protective of her son.

I knew it would help them for me to be up front.

"First, let me tell you what I do," I explained. "I sing songs and hymns to patients, and sometimes I read the Bible to them and pray for them."

"That's all right," the father said. "Tim could use some of that."

He told me that Tim had just turned eighteen when he was in a car accident. Right up to that time, he added, Tim had been growing increasingly rebellious. In fact, he hadn't been getting along with his parents for some time. He'd also been experimenting with drugs and dabbling in the occult.

I looked more closely at Tim. This boy was a wreck of a human being. Like many head-injured patients, his hands had curled up so that they looked deformed. His feet had turned almost completely outward. He had been a good wrestler in high school, his father told me, and Tim's body still showed traces of the stocky build he used to excel in that sport. I could tell he had once been a strong kid.

"Hi, Tim," I said. "My name's John. I'm going to sing some songs right now and invite God's Spirit to come into the room here with us. I think he's got something to speak to your heart that maybe I can't express in words."

I took my guitar out of the case. After a quick practice strum, I began to sing.

Immediately, a wall seemed to go up in Tim. And the more I sang, the more hardened he seemed to become. At first, he turned his head away from me. But I just kept singing and playing. This was nothing like my time with other patients. This kid Tim was one tough cookie.

When I was finished, his parents thanked me. I wasn't sure, but I hoped they couldn't tell how dazed I was by the experience. I packed up and went to see the other patients, wondering if I would get to see Tim again.

Despite Tim's cold response, I added him to my growing list of patients to see each week. Yet every time I went to Tim's room to sing to him, the same thing happened. He put up all the same walls and even tried to do things with his body to show he was ignoring me. Sometimes he flailed his arms and legs in what seemed to me a rage, and he uttered wild groans. He seemed to be resisting something.

I couldn't understand it. Yet I did my best to remain faithful. Week after week, month after month, I continued to see Tim. But in all that time, his response never changed.

During those early months at Milford, I remained very low-key in my approach. For the most part, I still didn't ask people about the possibility of singing to their injured loved ones. I did my best to stay true to what I felt was my calling—to be faithful and to wait on God. But it took a lot of faith—more faith than I felt I had at times—to believe he would someday open the doors that then seemed closed.

One of the reasons I felt this way was because the need at Milford was so great. There was virtually no ministry of any kind going on in the hospital.

I was deeply saddened by all the patients I saw there. Some wheeled themselves aimlessly down a hall. Others sat motionless in a hallway or an activity room. Still others lay in bed—with MTV or a rock radio station blaring, or soap operas playing continuously on a television overhead. (As the years have gone by, I've learned these are often typical scenarios in head-trauma centers.)

I tried to be hopeful whenever I saw the director of volunteers—*Please, Lord, let her have someone else for me to see today* ... But most of the time she didn't. And the work I did have was becoming more difficult. Of those few patients I was allowed to visit, very few regularly remained in their room. They were always being wheeled out for therapy or some other conflict or interruption.

I was particularly concerned about one patient named Bill. Bill's physical condition was bad—as bad as Tim's. I'd been given permission to see him, but every time I tried, he'd be snatched up by a nurse or an orderly and taken to therapy. I tried every way I could think of to see Bill—peeking into his room whenever I had a break between appointments or cutting my lunch short to hurry to his room. But something always came up, and I was never able to connect with him.

One day, as I was singing to Tim, I received a surprise. Another patient was wheeled into the room with Tim. His name was Don, and he was Tim's new roommate.

Don was nineteen—a handsome kid, from the pictures I saw of him: dark hair, olive complexion, perhaps of Italian descent. But now his body and limbs were gnarled and horribly contorted like Tim's. His condition was terrible.

Often when I went to visit Tim, I shared the gospel with Don as well. I told him about Jesus' work of salvation, and I prayed for him several times. I never got any real response from Don—none that I could tell, anyway. But at least he wasn't resistant, the way Tim was. I just couldn't tell whether I was getting through.

Then one Thursday, I suddenly felt the need to focus solely on Don. This time, I could see in his eyes that he was absorbing everything. I ended the time by praying for Don's salvation and leading him in prayer. I asked him to pray along with me in his heart.

The next Tuesday, as I was on my way to Tim and Don's room, a nurse stopped me in the hall. She touched my arm tenderly.

"John—" She cleared her throat. "Don died yesterday."

A lump rose in my throat. I was so grateful I'd followed my hunch to spend that one-on-one time with him. I knew I would miss him.

And I thought of one of the lessons I've learned over the years from the voiceless: *Some people are healed by going home.*

During the long drive home that day, I felt peaceful about Don. I had nothing to base that peace on—no physical evidence, no verbal evidence, not even a blink. But what I sensed in my heart was enough. In this work, I've learned you truly have to walk by faith and not by sight.

Little did I know at the time, though, the "sight" part would come soon enough.

I had been visiting Tim at Milford for a year and a half—still with no response—when his parents had to move him to another hospital for surgery. I found out from them later that Tim had almost died after the operation. When they brought him back to Milford, I decided to see him right away.

When I walked into the room, Tim was sitting upright in a wheelchair. I could tell he had lost a lot of weight.

"Hi Tim," I said. "It's John. You remember me, don't you?"

"No."

Huh? His response startled me. I looked closer to try to gauge Tim's expression. His gaze met mine directly.

What was this all about? Tim had never responded to me before—ever. In fact, I'd never known him to respond verbally to anyone. What's more, he had answered me in a clear, precise tone. By every indication, he was fully aware of what was taking place.

Yet, if he's this aware, I thought, *I'm surprised he doesn't remember me.*

"Are you sure you don't remember me, Tim?" I asked. "I've been coming to see you for a year and a half."

"No," he answered. Suddenly I recognized the old defiance. He even turned his head away from me slightly.

Yep—same old Tim. Maybe he recognized me after all and still didn't want to be bothered.

Nah! I told myself. *Maybe that head-jerk away from me was just a muscle reflex.*

"Well, I've come to see you again, Tim," I said, "and I want to play some music for you. I also want to pray for you and read some Scripture. Is that okay with you?"

"Yes."

Gulp. *Yes? Tim? Hello? Is that really you?*

I looked into his eyes again: His expression was clear. Yet I was puzzled: *What's he thinking?*

All I knew was, *John, here's your chance*. And I began to worship:

> *Blessed be the name of the Lord . . .*
> *Blessed be the name,*
> *Blessed be the name of the Lord.*

I began the chorus again with my eyes open, so I could watch Tim.

His eyes were riveted to mine. And his head was slightly tilted, almost an inquiring look. *What's going on inside you, Tim?*

Whatever it was, I knew it had to be good. Tim had never responded this way before, and I sensed a door was opening in his heart.

Just as I finished the second chorus, someone knocked on the door. I stopped playing.

A nurse peeked in.

"Hi," she said. "There's someone sitting here right outside your door, listening. Do you mind if I bring him in?"

"Not at all," I said.

The nurse took a moment to open the door, then wheeled the patient in. To my surprise, it was Bill—the guy I'd been trying to see for months!

"Hi, Bill!" I shouted.

"You know Bill?" the nurse asked. "Good, because he's just had his room assignment switched. He's going to be in here with Tim."

I could hardly believe my ears.

I began singing again, and after another chorus, the door opened once more and another nurse walked in. This time I just kept on worshiping. I was afraid she wanted to take either Bill or Tim out for therapy, and I knew we weren't finished yet.

What happened next surprised me. The nurse stepped up beside my chair—and she began singing along with me. My heart leapt as we both sang together:

> *As the deer panteth for the water*
> *So my soul longeth after thee;*
> *You alone are my heart's desire*
> *And I long to worship thee.*
> *You alone are my strength, my shield,*
> *To you alone does my spirit yield;*
> *You alone are my heart's desire,*
> *And I long to worship thee.*

The atmosphere in the room was indescribable.

I looked at Tim, and I saw tears forming in his eyes. This tough, young guy had never once shown any emotion before, much less tenderness. Now, obviously, something was touching him.

The nurse who had stepped in to accompany me left during the next chorus. After I finished singing, I put down my guitar.

"Tim," I asked, "do you sense the presence of God right now?"

He shook his head no.

"Well, you can," I said. "If you want to, you can ask him to come into your life. You can ask him to forgive you of your sins. Do you want to do that?"

He nodded—yes.

Yes. Yes!

I began sharing everything I knew of Christ's gift of salvation. I told both Tim and Bill of Jesus' great love for us, of the price he'd paid for us on the Cross, and of the wonderful future we could share with him for eternity.

I looked at Bill, but because of his condition, he couldn't respond. Then I turned to Tim. Tears were now running down his face.

"Bill, Tim—I'd like to pray with both of you," I said. "You may not be able to say what I do with words. But just pray from your heart. Jesus can hear you."

I began a prayer of repentance and salvation.

When we finished, I opened my eyes and looked at Tim.

"Tim, did you pray that prayer with me?"

The answer came slowly: "Yes."

"Did you ask Jesus to forgive you of your sins?"

A pause. Then, "Yes." His gaze on me was still steady.

"Did you ask him into your heart?"

Another pause. "Yes."

I could feel my heart in my throat. I was utterly amazed at what God had done. Yet I knew this was just the beginning.

"Listen, Tim," I began, "you're going to have to trust Jesus every day for the strength to get through all of this. You too, Bill. Tim, will you pray every day to Jesus?"

This time the pause was shorter. Then the answer came: "Yes."

Yes.

After that day, every time I walked into Tim's room, his face lit up. He obviously was happy to see me, and I was certainly happy to see him. The change in his countenance was remarkable. And it was evident to all the nurses and orderlies who worked with him. Several of them commented to me on the difference they'd seen in him.

Yet every week, I could tell that Tim had been worn down spiritually since I'd last visited him. Part of that might have been discouragement over his condition. It might have been the despair that naturally occurs whenever anyone's body works against them.

Yet I also reminded myself that Tim was just a baby Christian. And, in spite of his head injury, he had to do battle just like the rest of us. In fact, maybe even more so, because of his condition. He had to grow, struggle, and mature like every other person who's ever trusted in Jesus.

Another of Tim's problems was that he had no control over his environment. He couldn't control his TV, which was usually turned to the Weather Channel, or some other boring or inane subject. It must have been for that reason, I thought, that he always looked forward to our times together.

"So, Tim," I asked him once, "are you still praying to Jesus for strength?"

"Yes," he answered, his eyes fixed on me. Gone was the rebellious spirit, the rejecting turn of his head. Now, whenever I spoke to Tim, I had his total attention. And I liked to think those steely blue eyes were looking straight through me and on to Jesus, for the help he needed.

"Is Jesus answering your prayers?"

Tim's answer was slow but sure: "Yes."

Yes. What a beautiful word.

Especially when spoken by the voiceless.

I know it takes every ounce of strength inside for guys like Tim to keep going—to keep "putting one foot in front of the other," even if they can't do it physically. And I've come to recognize that Tim and others like him face the same tiring battles we all do: boredom, hopelessness, great spiritual need.

Like many of us, they find themselves faced every day by the same monotonous routines, the same struggles and heartaches. And they need God's kindness and love, and the love of others, in order to persevere.

We are all on this pilgrimage of faith together. And just as we do, the voiceless "desire a better country, that is a heavenly one. Therefore God is not ashamed to be called their God, for he has prepared a city for them" (Hebrews 11:16 ESV).

These voiceless young guys have spoken to me in a deep, special way. They're living reminders to me of words that are familiar to all of us:

Walk by faith, and not by sight.

No matter what the journey is.

Learning the Songs of Heaven: Living Eternity Now

6

All too often I've felt completely inadequate as I've spoken to families in crisis, families who have no voice. I have to admit to them up front, "I don't pretend to know what you're feeling. I can't begin to understand the pain you're going through. All I know is, Jesus does. He knows all about your pain. And he can touch you where no person can."

I accept by faith that God can meet their deepest needs. That faith is actually required for my work, day in and day out. The simple truth is, I often can't discern what people's deep, inner needs are. In fact, most of the time, I feel like I'm just on the outside looking in.

Then one day in 1993, that all began to change for Gail and me. We didn't know it, but we were about to find out for ourselves what it means to become voiceless.

How could any father or mother ever forget the date? July 13, 1990—that was the day our lives changed forever. Our beautiful firstborn child, John Samuel Wessells III, was born. The birth of this little boy brought us joy I'd never dreamed possible. He truly was a gift from heaven, one who would change everything about our lives—our marriage, our relationship with God, our relationship with the comatose.

At a certain stage in Gail's pregnancy, our nurse-midwife had pointed out that the baby inside Gail's womb could actually hear us talking and singing. We jokingly wondered if this child would be born already knowing the songs we sang in the hospitals to the comatose patients.

Soon after John Samuel arrived, we saw evidence of what the midwife had told us. On the day we brought him home from the hospital, Gail and I decided to have our first time of worship together with our new baby.

As I brought out my guitar, John Samuel was in his mother's arms, facing away from me. Yet, as soon as I began to strum, he immediately turned his little head in my direction. He seemed to focus in on the sound he'd heard many times before. Now he could finally see it!

From day one, John Samuel was sensitive to worship music. And it remained that way for him. It seemed that God had given us not only a beautiful son, but one who rejoiced along with us in the life we'd chosen.

Little John Sammy loved going with us to visit Keith and Mama Jane at the Cortland facility. He had a natural love for people who were hurting. When he was just three, he looked up at Gail and declared, "Mama, when I get older, I'm going to go to the hospitals and sing with Daddy. And you'll stay home and make us supper." How I longed for the day when that would happen.

Both Gail and I constantly found ourselves learning from our son—learning important lessons of love and faith. In fact, it was through John Samuel that I learned of a father's unconditional love for his child, and a child's unconditional love for his father. Everything about this little boy touched both of our lives.

One hot August evening, just a month after his third birthday, John Samuel came to his mom complaining of stomach pain. Gail checked and saw that he was running a low-grade fever. When I got home, we decided to take John Samuel to an emergency room. We loaded up in the van and drove to Lourdes Hospital, twenty-five minutes away in Binghamton, New York.

The doctors looked John Samuel over and checked out a few things. Finally, X-rays were ordered, and the waiting game began. A while later, the doctor came back with the results: nothing serious, we were told, just a bad case of constipation.

Whew. Gail and I looked at each other and breathed a sigh of relief.

"That was scary," I said. "I think I'm getting a better feel for what the families at the head-injury hospitals go through."

Then the next day, we received a call from the radiologist at Lourdes.

"Mr. Wessells," he asked, "do you realize your son has pneumonia?"

What? Pneumonia?

"It seems they shot the X-ray of his stomach a little higher than usual," he explained. "We're seeing now that there's a spot on his lower left lung. We need you to come in right away."

How could this be? I thought. *He isn't coughing or showing any signs of having pneumonia. There must be a mistake.*

When we arrived at the hospital, we were shown John Samuel's X-ray. Sure enough, there appeared to be a spot. The doctors continued to call it pneumonia and said we shouldn't worry. They could start John Samuel on an antibiotic right away; that should take care of the problem and clear it up within seven to ten days.

Everything went fine until a week later, when John Samuel again complained about stomach pain. Once more, Gail checked him and found he had a high fever. We immediately rushed him to the hospital again. This time, X-rays showed that the pneumonia had spread to nearly half of his left lung. John Samuel would have to be hospitalized now and put on intravenous antibiotics to kill the infection.

Nothing in my life had prepared me for the pain I felt next. I had to hold down my three-year-old son on the examining table so a nurse could insert an IV into his hand. It was my most traumatic test as a father. As I looked into his frightened eyes, I think I felt as helpless and out of control as he must have felt.

Four days later, we were on our way back home. Finally, things with our son seemed to be under control. There was no more fever—in fact, no sign of any problem at all. Yet Gail and I had quickly learned what it felt like to be overprotective parents. Before leaving the hospital, we asked about possibly having another X-ray taken. We just wanted to make sure everything was cleared up.

The doctor assured us that an X-ray wasn't necessary. It wouldn't reflect any improvement for several days. He advised us to see our regular pediatrician in five days, and we could do a follow-up exam then.

We did just that. When we met with the pediatrician, Gail and I were assured things were looking good for John Samuel. Yet I just couldn't rest easily without having a final look at an X-ray. So I asked for one again to put my mind at ease.

The doctor smiled and told us there was no reason for that. "When you come back in two weeks for your follow-up exam, we'll do an X-ray then," the doctor explained. But the X-ray never happened.

Three days before we were scheduled to see the doctor again, John Samuel had another fever. Now we were starting to get really frustrated. I called the pediatrician, but again I was told not to worry. He said this was normal at the end of a bout with pneumonia, that we should just wait to see him at our scheduled appointment in three days.

The next day, when I got home from the head-injury hospital, I noticed John Samuel sitting lifelessly on the couch. He was panting and sweating.

"Gail, this boy is sick!" I said.

"We've been waiting forever for you to get home," Gail said desperately. "He's been like this for hours."

"Come on, we're going to the emergency room," I said. "We're not waiting for tomorrow's appointment."

We both knew something was wrong. Now we were really fearful. When we arrived at the emergency room, Gail and I were almost hysterical.

Once again, an X-ray was taken. This time, everyone in the emergency room seemed to be rushing in to look at John Samuel's X-ray. Finally, I stole a peek myself.

What's the big deal? I thought. The picture was completely white. I couldn't see anything on it.

We soon learned why the picture was all white. It was because John Samuel's lungs and chest cavity were filled with fluid. In fact, it had caused his heart to move all the way to the right side of his body. His trachea tube, which normally was vertical, was now diagonally positioned under his collarbone.

This news began a whirlwind of events. We were hurriedly loaded into an ambulance and whisked off to another hospital. At that point we weren't told anything about John Samuel's condition. I can vaguely remember a nurse from the ER looking into the ambulance, handing me John Samuel's X-rays and saying, "Mr. Wessells, your son is really sick."

Within minutes, we arrived at Wilson Memorial Hospital and were escorted to a patient room. John Samuel was put into bed, where he lay quietly in a hospital gown and socks, with an oxygen tube strapped to his nose. Sitting at his bedside, I finally started sobbing uncontrollably. I was blaming myself for not taking action sooner. Now it felt as if the entire weight of the world was on my shoulders. I kept telling myself, *I should have insisted on that X-ray.*

Then, I felt a gentle touch on my cheek. When I looked up, I saw it was John Samuel's little foot. He had lifted his leg and was drying my tears with his hospital sock. Without speaking a word, he was staring calmly into my eyes. I knew he was trying to say, *Daddy, it's going to be all right. It's not your fault. I love you!*

I looked at him and said, "Little boy, I love you. I promise you, I'm going to do everything to make sure you get better."

A short time later, we were told that John Samuel's condition was more serious than they could handle at Wilson. He would have to be transferred to University Hospital in Syracuse, New York. Once more, John Samuel was put into the back of an ambulance. Only this trip wouldn't be for just a few minutes. It would be an hour-and-a-half long.

Gail rode with our son in the emergency vehicle, while I tried to keep up in our van. It had begun to rain, and the night was unusually dark. Soon the rain was falling hard, and visibility was poor due to the huge raindrops pummeling my windshield. Eventually, I became separated from the ambulance.

At that moment, I felt separated from everyone and everything, even God. I cried out to him, but the silence of his response was deafening. My life seemed totally out of control, in a way I'd never felt before.

It seemed to take forever to get to the hospital. When I finally arrived, it was 2 a.m. Gail was relieved to see me, because there were so many doctors, students, and nurses hovering around John Samuel's bed. Two hours later, they decided on a surgical procedure. They would have to insert tubes into John Samuel's chest cavity to drain the fluid and relieve the incredible amount of pressure that had caused one of his lungs to collapse. His other lung was only functioning at 50-percent capacity.

Due to the urgency of the need for the procedure, the doctors decided to do it right away, there in the room. But they wouldn't be able to sedate John Samuel because of his impeded breathing. As the staff scurried about the room, preparing to make the first incision, the doctor turned to me and said, "Mr. Wessells, you and your wife will have to step outside."

We protested, but everyone assured us it was absolutely necessary. Little John Samuel began crying, "Daddy, Mama, don't leave me, please, don't leave me!"

I can't find words to describe the next forty-five minutes, as we stood outside the door of that room. Our three-year-old boy continued screaming in pain, as two chest tubes were inserted in his side without any anesthesia or pain killers. All Gail and I could do was sob and pray, sob and pray.

When it was finally over, John Samuel's breathing seemed 100 percent better. And he was able to rest comfortably. For us, just then, the worst seemed to be over.

But the next twenty-four hours brought high, spiking fevers that were virtually unmanageable. John Samuel's temperature would leap several degrees within minutes. And there seemed to be no rhyme or reason for this. *What is going on, God?* I wondered. *This seems so chaotic, so uncontrollable, so . . . unreal.*

At some point during that roller-coaster ride of emotions, I thought back to some of the families of head-injured patients we knew. Their comatose loved ones had endured sudden, high fevers also. And they'd had to face roller coasters of their own, without a moment's notice.

Yet there was another similarity I was slowly seeing. That is, when I told those families that I didn't understand what they were going through, I was absolutely right. The view from this side of the bed was a totally different one. And it was a terribly lonely place to be.

People often asked me how I was able to handle singing to head-trauma patients due to the catastrophic nature of the injuries. They couldn't imagine themselves sitting next to someone in a severe head-injured state for any length of time without falling apart.

I always answered that I had the easy part. I would come and sing for a few hours, then go home and leave the situation behind, along with much of the pain involved. I pointed out that the parents were the people who should be asked that question. They carried their pain with them seven days a week, twenty-four hours a day.

Now I realized that even this was a vast understatement. Nothing could have prepared me for the pain of what we were going through with three-year-old John Samuel. And I could tell by the looks on the faces of those around us that there was nothing they could do in order to see *from the inside out.* To feel what we felt.

There was no let-up for us over the next few days. We saw more groups of doctors and more specialized-medicine groups than I'd ever thought existed. At times Gail and I had to step aside from the chaos and ask ourselves, *Why all these continuing questions? Isn't everything settled here? They told us it was just pneumonia that had run wild. Surely antibiotics will help now— won't they?*

Whenever the different groups of attending doctors came along, we heard them whispering things such as *cystic fibrosis, legionnaire's disease, lung cancer.* All of the possibilities seemed awful, some more than others. And all the highs and lows of simply *not knowing* turned our stomachs upside down, twisting them into knots.

Finally, a doctor came to John Samuel's room to introduce herself. She informed us of the need to do thorascopic surgery on John Samuel's left lung. And it had to be done the very next day, which was Labor Day.

We knew it was serious if they had to do surgery on a holiday weekend. The doctor's theory was that John Samuel had pneumonia that had run wild; now it had solidified in his lung, and it wasn't allowing the antibiotics to penetrate and kill the infection. It was necessary for them to clean out infectious mass . . . and, if necessary, remove the lung itself.

Remove the lung?

Only a parent would understand what Gail and I went through in that moment. All the dreams we'd had for our little boy went racing through our minds. And suddenly, every one of those dreams hung in the balance. Would his life still be possible as we had dreamed it? Could anyone—especially someone as young as John Samuel—lead a normal life with only one lung?

Before we could even grasp the questions, we were being handed consent papers. Our signatures would give the surgeons permission to remove John Samuel's lung if necessary.

Once again, we felt completely out of control.

Doctors say that the surgery John Samuel underwent that Labor Day weekend was one of the most painful there is. It took about five hours, and it would be as many days before our little boy recovered from the procedure. But the operation itself was accompanied by good news: Everything was a success. The doctors were able to remove all the infection. And they were able to save John Samuel's lung.

We were elated. Gail and I thanked God for his goodness to us, and his great mercy toward our son. Meanwhile, the doctor told us she would send out the infectious mass to be examined. She was confident it was nothing more than a solidified infection, but she wanted to make sure.

Five days later, we were ready to go home. I was packing up our things at the hotel where we were staying when the phone rang. Gail said I needed to come back to the hospital right away. It seems the doctor on the floor needed to talk to us together.

Once again, I felt the familiar drop of the roller coaster, going down, down, down. My stomach began to twist in knots.

I met Gail and we were led to a conference room full of doctors. As soon as we sat down, the head doctor began speaking. Her voice quavered as she said, "We have bad news for you. Your son's biopsy came back—and it shows he has cancer. What's worse, it's a very rare cancer. I'm—we're—very sorry."

This time, the big dip of the roller coaster took my breath away completely.

Pulmonary Blastoma—a tumor originating in the lining of the lung.

Only twenty-seven known cases. And very little data on effective approaches to treatment, if any at all.

It would be a guessing game for us.

Gail and I reacted exactly as we'd seen families of head-trauma patients do. We tried to get a second opinion from anyone who might be able to give us hope.

But just like those families, there was none to be found.

For the next fifteen months, we were thrown into an endless boot camp of emotions. We were now experiencing firsthand all the feelings we'd only witnessed from a distance before: Helplessness. Hopelessness. Powerlessness. Fearfulness. Fatigue. Depression. Despair. These were but a few.

We were also thrown into an entire other world, complete with its own terminology: Hickman catheter. Aggressive chemotherapy. White cell counts up. White cell counts down. What were these things? And what would they do to our child?

Neutropenic. Blood transfusions. Platelet transfusions. Spiked fevers. Line infections. Nuclear medicine. Neupogen shots. MRIs. CT Scans. Around every corner, there was a new, unfamiliar concept to grasp. And we had to make sure we grasped them all firmly right away.

Cisplatin. Adriamycin. Vincristine. Actinomycin. Cytoxan. We quickly found out that some of these names were more ominous than others. In fact, a few were almost like enemies, as opposed to friendly medicines that maybe, maybe, would bring a cure.

Most of the time, it was too much for us to take. Why was this happening to us? Gail and I woke up some days wondering if some kind of mistake had been made. *Please,* we each thought, *someone, tell me this is just a long nightmare. Somebody, wake me up from this.*

We'd had to make major decisions concerning our beloved son's treatment. Should we put him through the severe protocol that was being suggested? Very aggressive chemotherapy, with multiple surgeries? Were we willing to subject him to all the suffering this meant, because we didn't want to lose him?

At first, we were reluctant to put John Samuel through any more pain. He'd already been through so much. Besides, there wasn't much information available on complete remissions among the other twenty-seven patients. But we had to make a decision soon—now, in fact. The doctors were telling us that without treatment, our son had only a month to live. Whatever time we took to decide—a day or even a few hours—could be crucial to his survival.

How could we know whether we were making the right decision?

And how, I wondered, *could God ask this kind of decision of any parent?*

I had been asked the same questions by the families of brain-injured people. I never knew what to tell them. And now, I realized, I didn't know what to tell myself. All I knew was that I loved my son more than anything else in this world. I only wanted to do right by him.

While Gail and I agonized, our doctors found some statistics for Pulmonary Blastoma: There were four known survivors of this rare cancer.

Now we had to do some deep soul searching. Were we willing to do whatever we felt was right—regardless of whether that meant watching him undergo the agony of treatment or (a thought unthinkable at that point) releasing him from life on this earth to go and be with the Lord?

We realized there was one factor we couldn't rule out of our decision. Even though John Samuel had been put through tremendous pain and suffering up to that point, he still always seemed to find a way to live life to the fullest. No matter what agony he faced, he still looked forward to every day.

Now Gail and I wondered, *How could we not give our joyful little boy a chance to continue living his young life to the fullest? How could we not allow him to continue to fight, and perhaps even beat, the odds, as low as they might be?*

Our decision became final: We would go ahead with the suggested protocol. John Samuel would have a Hickman catheter surgically implanted in his chest to receive chemotherapy treatments. And those treatments would begin immediately.

Gail and I didn't know it, but we had entered a new realm we knew nothing about. A whole new set of questions rose for us with no one to answer them: How does chemotherapy work? Will John Samuel lose his hair? Will he be sick from these treatments? What are the long-term effects for him, if he should even make it that far?

Over the next several months, we would be faced with these questions and others like them every day.

That night, after our decision to move forward with chemotherapy, the phone rang. It was a couple, Rick and Sally Day, who asked if they could come see us and share a similar story they'd gone through with one of their daughters, Suzanne. Feeling completely alone in our dilemma, we welcomed the chance to hear the Days' story.

At one point in her own journey, young Suzanne Day was given less than a 10-percent chance of survival. Now, years later, she was as healthy as the moment she was born. Yet as the Days told us their daughter's story, they weren't trying to give us some kind of false hope. In fact, this deeply genuine couple didn't pretend to come to us with answers of any kind. But they did come with hearts of compassion and understanding. They comforted us with the same comfort they'd been given.

It was just what Gail and I needed.

We came to rely on such kindnesses. My anxiety was at an all-time high the day before John Samuel was scheduled to have his Hickman catheter implanted. It would mark the beginning of his first round of chemo.

Yet that same day, we received a postcard from an acquaintance. It was a man who had been through the same trial with his son.

He opened his heart to us, describing all the emotions we could relate to. He told us that as he sat by his son's bedside, watching the chemo run into his veins, never knowing what the outcome would be, he was able to endure. He didn't know how. He only knew that Jesus was there with him, his arms wrapped around them both.

John Samuel made it through his first round of chemo with minimal side effects. We were hopeful after that.

But the second round was different. The medications that John Samuel took this time made him violently ill. I felt my heart was being ripped right out of my chest as I held my son's vomit dish, trying to console him. All through the night, I watched my three-year-old boy grow sick and throw up, with only five-minute intervals of relief.

At one point during that long night, I seriously considered stopping all forms of treatment. I couldn't go on any longer watching him suffer. I tried not to cry in front of him, but finally I was no longer able to contain my tears. I kept praying to myself, "Lord, how long will I have to sit here and watch this precious boy suffer?" All night long, I'd felt an anger welling up inside me. Now it was beginning to boil over.

Just then, John Samuel said, "Daddy, look!"

He pointed out the window. There, beyond two tall cement buildings facing the hospital, was a small patch of sky. As I looked outside with him, I saw that the sun was about to rise. It was that certain moment of the day, with the sky the most beautiful color of midnight blue I'd ever seen. And there, up in that patch of blue, was a bright morning star. It looked as if it had been placed there by God himself, just for John Samuel.

"Look at the beautiful sky that Jesus made for me, Daddy," he said.

He was so excited, he could hardly contain himself.

"Oh, yeah, little boy," I marveled with him. "Look at what he did."

With that, John Samuel calmly turned his head back toward the bed and vomited.

I held him gently as he continued retching. I could barely take in what I was seeing. And I was broken by it.

Our little son had never complained once throughout this whole ordeal. And now, in the midst of his most intense suffering, he was able to look up and enjoy a glimpse of God's beauty.

Meanwhile, here I was, a worship leader, angry over the awful place that life had led me. But my son, even though he was in terrible pain, had his gaze fixed on the heavens. My little John Samuel thought only of God's love.

In the end, round two of chemotherapy proved effective in treating John Samuel's tumor. There was over a 75-percent shrinkage, much to the amazement of our doctors. It seemed we were on the road to recovery. Finally, after the fifth round of chemo, another surgery was necessary to clean up any remaining tumor.

The surgery went well, though again very painful. I still have the image of my son's little body lying on the gurney in the recovery room, crying from the intense pain he went through and looking for his daddy's hand to hold. With all of the tumor seemingly removed now, John Samuel faced four rounds of follow-up chemo to complete his treatment. We couldn't wait for it all to be over.

During that final treatment period, I couldn't help noticing that we were receiving fewer and fewer visitors and phone calls. It brought to me a new realization about my work with the comatose and their families. It showed me in a new way just how valuable my visits to those isolated people must have been.

It's such an indescribable blessing just to have someone come into your room and talk to you, even if it's only about superficial things. It breaks up the monotony of listening to all of the pumps and buzzers going off around the clock. Gail and I were also thankful for the Christians who came to our son's room and prayed with us. They probably didn't think they helped much, but they did. I began to realize that more was probably going on during my times with the head-injured and their families than I realized.

Many of us stay away from suffering people because we're not really sure what to say, what to give. But I realize now that it's enough to just *be* with them. That's something we all can do.

During this lonely period for us, we received an unexpected gift from Gail's father. He lived in Florida, but for years he'd owned some land on a mountain nearby us. Now he wanted to give the property to us, in hopes that we might be able to build a house on it someday.

Gail and I were overjoyed at this incredible gift. And it couldn't have come at a better time. We knew it would lift John Samuel's spirits to think of having a home on a mountaintop. So together we all started dreaming out loud about it.

In between his final rounds of chemo, when John Sammy was feeling healthy and strong, we drove our van to the mountain where the lot stood. It became a place of utter freedom for our son, as he romped through the grass, making up songs and singing loudly to God. We all hiked together up to the crest of the slope, where the property line was. And the whole time, John Sammy talked endlessly about our land.

Gail always beamed whenever John Sammy was so happy. "Isn't it wonderful, John Samuel?" she said during one of his romps. "Our family is going to have a house here one day."

John Samuel stopped playing. He turned to listen to her intently.

"You're going to have a nice big yard to play in," Gail added. "And a swing set. And you and Daddy will get to hike up to the top every day."

John Samuel thought about this. Then, in a soft tone, he said, "But, Mama, it will only be our house for a little while. Our real home is in heaven."

Gail and I looked at each other, puzzled. We weren't sure why he said this. We only knew he seemed convinced of it.

I was excited as I signed what I thought would be John Samuel's last set of discharge papers. As I packed up our son's things before taking him home, I told him, "John Samuel, you're all finished with chemo. Now you're all better. Soon your hair will grow back, and they'll take out your Hickman catheter!"

He looked at me with his usual gentle little smile and said, "Daddy, I'm not all better. But that's okay."

His words took me aback.

"What do you mean, son?" I asked. "You're all through with chemo, and you're all better."

He just smiled and didn't say anything.

His response was sobering to me, and puzzling. Did he know something I didn't?

Suddenly, I remembered a time some nine months before, when John Samuel began singing songs he'd made up on his little makeshift guitar (a ukulele). I remember wondering at the time, *Why is he singing so much about going to heaven?*

He would always sing his songs with words like, "Go in heaven to see, go in heaven to see, with God your Father there, you will be all right. Let's go to our salvation." And "God, I want to go with you, yes I do, yes I do, God I want to go with you to heaven."

I didn't want to hear him sing about going to heaven. So I put it out of my mind at the time. All I could think about during his chemotherapy was my son getting better and our family living happily ever after.

John Samuel's focus on heaven might have unsettled me for the moment. But our family was looking forward to celebrating something in the coming days. We were all excitedly awaiting the arrival of our second child, who was due any day. In fact, the day after we returned from our last round of chemo, Gail went into labor and gave birth to a 7-pound, 14-ounce baby girl, Daniele Elizabeth Wessells.

John Samuel was thrilled at the idea of having a little sister to look after. This seemed to be an appropriate end to our long crisis. Now we could get on with our lives and our new family.

However, this too was short-lived.

Three weeks later, at John Samuel's next follow-up checkup, the doctors discovered a new growth in the same lining of his lung. This meant that the tumor had been growing through at least the last two rounds of chemo. It wasn't a good sign.

Once again, our hopes were being shaken to the core. This would mean yet another surgery, and yet another game plan for treatment.

How would we ever break the news to our son, who had bravely endured so much at three years of age? Or, at what point should we just say, "Enough is enough"?

We had no idea.

The surgery wasn't as long as the others, but it seemed to take its toll on John Samuel. He didn't bounce back as fast as he did after the two previous surgeries.

At that point, I felt I couldn't endure one more day of watching him lie there in pain. All the stress of the ordeal was taking its toll on all of us. And now we had the responsibility of a newborn baby to take care of. Gail and I had never felt so exhausted.

And once again, we faced tough decisions regarding our son's treatment. The procedure that the doctors had originally planned before his surgery wasn't possible anymore, because now there was a large amount of scar tissue on his lungs. We were running out of options and time.

The holidays were quickly approaching, but it was impossible for us to focus on anything other than John Samuel. He was due for a new X-ray just before Thanksgiving, but I asked if it could wait until the Monday afterward. I just wanted our family to be able to enjoy the holidays. But then, maybe I just wanted to put off more bad news.

The X-ray couldn't wait.

And the news was the worst it could possibly be.

We were told by his doctor that our son had two to four weeks to live. Two months, tops.

Gail and I both just started crying. We knew we were out of options.

We were asked if we wanted to try more experimental drugs, but we decided that enough was enough. Either God would miraculously heal him, or John Samuel was going home to be with him.

How do you live, knowing you're sitting on a time bomb waiting to go off? And that explosion involves your child?

We kept getting regular X-rays, so we could keep abreast of the tumor's growth. With each examination, we were hoping that somehow, miraculously, the tumor would be gone. But it only continued to grow.

Finally, at our doctor's suggestion, we decided to do radiation treatments. We knew it would only prolong the inevitable. But we wanted to try to get John Samuel through the Christmas holidays.

After his second round of radiation, we asked for a CT scan to see if there were any other problems that might be causing his pain. We were in one of the examining rooms, anxiously awaiting the results, when I heard our doctor paged to the radiology department. At that point, my heart was racing, and I was gripped by fear. For forty-five minutes I paced the room like a caged animal, waiting to see the doors swing open and the doctor walk in.

Finally, the doctor arrived. He had that all-too-familiar look of disappointment on his face. He said sympathetically, "They found two large tumors on your son's brain. I'm very sorry."

We had been fighting for fifteen months. Now I didn't feel any fight left in me.

John Samuel lay on the bed listening to the doctor. He didn't flinch at the news. And he never asked Gail or me if he was going to die. The doctor suggested that we admit him to the hospital to get his morphine adjusted to a comfortable level. Then we would be able to bring him home for Christmas.

I thought back to past Christmases. This season was always one of John Samuel's favorite times of year. He had always begun to get excited about Christmas just as Thanksgiving was approaching. Despite his condition, this Christmas was no different for him. He was as excited as ever, especially now that he had a baby sister.

Several weeks earlier, our family had been at a mall doing some shopping. John Samuel and I were looking for presents for little Daniele, while his mommy went shopping for us. As the people all around us were rushing around, caught up in the hustle and bustle of the holidays, John Samuel seemed to be caught up in the true meaning of Christmas. I watched him as he danced and sang his way down the center of the mall, seemingly unconscious of anyone else around him.

At one point, he sang his favorite song from the "Donut Man" Christmas video: "The best present of all is Jesus; the best present of all is God's son; Oh, the best present of all is the one who died for us, yes, the best present of all is from him." I could tell by people's expressions that the words seemed to be sinking in, if only for a brief moment.

Now, I so wanted us to spend Christmas at home again together. Gail and I were determined to do everything we could to see that happen, if only for a day. So, John Samuel and I talked about Christmas—it would be here in just four days!— as we sat at the hospital, while he received his increase in morphine to help him endure the pain through the next day.

That night, I spent the night in the hospital room with John Sammy while Gail traveled back home with little Daniele. The next morning when he woke, John Samuel wasn't very talkative, due to his increase in morphine. But we had a lot of visitors that day, and John Sammy was happy to see them all. Later, he suggested we have a family night with the friends who'd come and watch videos together. We all agreed.

We put in another of his favorite "Donut Man" videos, "Resurrection Celebration." John Samuel wanted to make sure everyone paid close attention, especially our friend Louisa. Whenever she turned away even for a second, John Samuel looked straight at her and said, "Louisa, you're not watching!"

After a while, he began to drift in and out of consciousness. I could tell he was slowly entering into a noncommunicative stage. At about midnight, long after everyone had left, I tried to tuck him in and say goodnight, but he didn't respond.

I lay down in my chair and tried to get some more rest, knowing we had a big day ahead of us. I had to be ready to take him home for Christmas.

⟡

I was awakened by the sound of his laughter. At first I chuckled at the sound. Then I realized he might be hallucinating from the amount of drugs he'd been given. Or, maybe he was just having a funny dream. Finally, I sensed he was seeing something that seemed very real to him. He was saying things such as, "There's Winnie the Pooh. And good ol' Piglet!" He talked about some of the imaginary friends he'd grown close to. He seemed happy, almost euphoric.

Then, suddenly, he sat up quickly and asked, "Daddy, Daddy, is it morning?"

I couldn't figure out why he would think that, since the room was pitch black. I answered, "I don't think so, John Samuel. Let me get my watch and see."

I held my watch up to the night-light.

"No, it's only 2:30. It's not morning yet."

He kept asking me, "Are you sure it's not morning? When will it be morning?"

I suddenly realized he was talking as normally as ever. And his eyes were extremely bright.

The next day I might have wakened wondering if this had happened at all. But John Samuel's night nurse, Andy, had come in, and stood by in amazement with me as he listened to our conversation.

I had never seen John Samuel so happy. All I could think was that God was answering my prayers and healing him. It brought great comfort to see my son like this.

We talked for about ten minutes. His eyes were as clear as I've ever seen them. There wasn't any sign of his being on high doses of morphine or having any kind of pain whatsoever. I thought to myself, *It's going to be a great Christmas after all. I knew God would come through.*

Finally, I had to cut our conversation short.

"John Samuel," I pointed out, "we need to get some rest. Remember, tomorrow we're going home for Christmas."

At that, he reached his arms up around my neck and squeezed me tightly. "Okay, Daddy," he answered. "Good night. I love you, and I'll see you in the morning!"

Then he lay back down and went into a deep sleep.

The next morning, I was gathering up our things and preparing to sign the discharge papers. John Samuel still appeared to be in a deep sleep.

But as I began to dress him, I could tell his legs were getting stiff and his feet were becoming distended. As many times as I've seen such symptoms with the brain-injured, I knew all too well what this meant. The tumor was pressing on the control center of his brain. Everything was beginning to shut down.

I continued to try to put his shirt on, but I could tell my son was dying. I fell by the bedside and began to cry, pleading with God for his life. Finally, I said to the nurse, "Please, get the doctor. My son's dying. I'm not going to be taking him home."

The doctor arrived shortly. She confirmed what I'd thought.

I phoned Gail and told her to come right away. Our friends began to arrive also, and we gathered around John Samuel's bed, praying and singing. It was the only comfort we could find.

Soon John Samuel's breathing became noticeably heavier. His life was slipping away.

Then, all of a sudden, he began reaching his hands toward us. We thought he wanted to hold our hands. But as we reached out to take hold of him, his hands continued past ours, reaching outward as if to heaven.

His eyes slowly started to open. Now John Sammy was murmuring something. We were stunned, because before now he had been totally paralyzed from the brain tumor. One doctor's only explanation for this afterward was, "He must have seen the angels coming for him."

Shortly after that, John Samuel put his hands down and breathed his last breath. It was December 23, 1994—two days before Christmas.

The silence in the room was deafening. Yet there was a peace I cannot explain. Gail and I both knew and could sense that John Samuel had been ushered into the presence of Jesus.

We'd always told our doctors we were confident that, no matter what happened, John Samuel would be safe in Jesus' arms. Now our main concern was how we would be able to live without him.

We simply didn't want to leave the room. How do you just walk away and leave your child, knowing you'll never see him again in this lifetime?

For four-and-a-half years—and especially during the pre-ceding sixteen months—I had taken my son wherever he needed to go and had done with him whatever needed to be done. Now, I was being relieved of all my natural, instinctive duties as his father. And I didn't know how to do that.

I was entering into a whole new world. I've never known such pain, or such peace.

Some things are too deep to be voiced.

One of the first things I realized in the following days was that John Samuel was finally, truly . . . *seeing*. What he'd heard in the womb and responded to on his first day home, as we sang worship songs, he was now seeing.

Seeing the promise that's held out for all who believe.

What he'd seen through a glass darkly during his life with us, he was now seeing face-to-face.

That truth—the truth that our son was now seeing fully what he'd sensed throughout his lifetime—has been a great source of comfort to Gail and me. And we also have another source of comfort: We now have a family of five—including Daniele, Rachel, and David—who look forward to one day meeting their brother.

We're fully aware that our lives will never be "normal," the way we knew it before. We don't have any illusions about that. But then, for any family who's lost a child, life can *never* get "back to normal." That's because what's happened to them isn't meant to be forgotten.

What's important is the legacy.

John Samuel left us an important legacy, one that speaks loudly for the voiceless. I sum it up this way:

My son sang the songs of heaven while still on earth. He made up songs about the *eternal,* while living in the *now.* He looked forward to a better place—even while living fully in the place he was in.

I believe that's the hope for all of us who want to listen to the voiceless. Nothing may change in our circumstances, or in the circumstances of those we love. But it is still possible, as it was for my son, to live with eternity in our eyes and hearts. And that changes everything.

It's still possible to sing the songs of heaven.

When There Are No Words, There's Music

7

Music has always been intensely personal to me. When I first started picking up the guitar at age eight, I would close the door to my room and just play. I was free then, because I knew no one else was listening. Music expressed the deepest, most wordless parts of my soul. It gave me a voice.

When I became a Christian in my mid-twenties, I found a direct connection to God through music. Suddenly, I had an added purpose for singing. Not only could I express the depths of my heart, but I could interact with the Creator of the universe. I used music to worship the Lord, and I always got something in return. It was a way to enter deeper into my relationship with him, to celebrate it and enjoy it.

It has been said that music is the universal language. I've found that to be true in every realm where I've seen music used.

In the years after the Iron Curtain fell, I took several trips with various groups to Romania. I remember that first trip well. Changes were happening fast in that country, and situations were constantly in flux. Our group had to adapt quickly to different scenarios, and we did almost everything on the fly.

At one point, a local leader in the town of Kluj had rented a movie theater for us to use. We were scheduled to hold evangelistic meetings there for the public. That first evening, it was ninety-five degrees, and the theater had no air conditioning, but the place was packed anyway. The children had to be taken outside for a separate meeting to make more room in the theater for the adults.

Our group arrived just before the meeting was supposed to start. Suddenly we realized we had a translator for the speaker but not for the music. Someone suggested we write out the lyrics in Romanian, but we didn't have time or the means to do it.

We had no words.

We realized all we could do was sing in the language we knew. And we had to trust the music to translate itself.

We'd barely made it through the first verse when we saw people in the audience weeping. Then they began to cry things out loud. *What was this all about?* I wondered. As far as I could tell, they couldn't understand a word we sang. I finally asked our translator what they were saying.

"They're crying out to Jesus," he said. "They want him to save them."

Music's universal language is especially true in my work with the comatose. It doesn't matter what kind of situation a family may be facing. They might be hoping in vain for their child's healing. They could be agonizing over whether to stop life-support. They might be growing more rigid and unyielding, trying to regain some measure of control over their lives. I've seen people in each of these situations. And, in each case, I've seen how music can touch the wordless parts of their souls.

Music can help us lay down the burdens we're carrying in the moment. I'm not talking about using music as an escape. Actually, just the opposite is true: music brings perspective. In the midst of the worst possible circumstances, I've seen music usher in peace, light, and hope. It can actually help us face reality more clearly.

Music is a reminder that no matter what we're going through, we're in the presence of one greater than ourselves, one who cares about all our wordless moments. All our voiceless moments.

Recording my CD *Tell Him for Me* was the best possible therapy I could have had. The title song applies to the comatose, but I wrote it about our son John Samuel. I wanted Jesus to tell John Sammy all the things I couldn't. The ongoing grief that Gail and I felt from day to day was relentless.

Recording *Tell Him for Me* was a way to move forward through what had just happened to us. I was forced to face issues and to sing about them, even on the days when I barely had energy to speak about them.

I realize now that *Tell Him for Me* wasn't really about music at all. It was about surviving. And music was there to help me do just that. It helped me be "right where I was at." And it helped me face what I had to do to keep living. I know what it's like to feel voiceless in the deepest part of my being. Music spoke for me then.

Even when I couldn't play or sing myself, music reached out to me. Sometimes it came to us through friends. When we were at our lowest point, our friend Walter (who played cello so beautifully on the CD) picked up a guitar and simply sang Scripture songs. He'd probably played those same songs a thousand times before. But to Gail and me, it was as if we were hearing them for the first time. They made old truths new. They brought new hope and new life to us when we needed it most. Throughout this long journey of grief, music has been a healer for us. I'll always be thankful to God for it.

Music gets right to the heart of the matter without any detours. Gail and I have seen music work its power with the comatose and their families a thousand times. Just like in Romania, we often barely get through a single verse before we see tears beginning to flow. The people don't know how to describe what they're experiencing. They struggle for words, saying, "It's so soothing; it's so peaceful." Or, they attribute their experience to the playing or singing. Yet even then, they know that what they're feeling goes much deeper than any words could express.

The reason they're at a loss for words is that they're responding to something beyond themselves. To Gail and me, they've encountered the Spirit of God. They're being touched by something that's beyond their understanding. I always have to remind myself not to explain too much about what's happening in that moment. It's tempting to try to put words to it. The truth is, you don't have to tell people when they're experiencing the love of God. They know it.

If you asked me to describe what's happening in simple terms, I'd say faith is being born. And only God can do that in a person. My job is simply to sing the songs.

One of the first examples I saw of music's healing power was when I worked with a young patient named Mark. He was college aged, but because of his head injury, he had the mental capacity of a five- to seven-year-old. He couldn't speak very well, only a few words. And he could only move an arm and a leg.

Whenever I read Scriptures and sang to Mark, he seemed to hang right along with me. He couldn't respond verbally. But over time, in working with the comatose, I've learned to read patients' facial expressions. And Mark's told me he was soaking in everything. He especially enjoyed himself when I sang. He seemed to respond to one particular chorus, "Praise the Name of Jesus." Whenever I asked him if he understood what I was talking or singing about, he nodded.

Yet I knew Mark had a hard time with his memory. Every week when I came to see him, he couldn't remember anything we'd done the week before. It all seemed new to him each time. Sometimes he couldn't even remember who I was. It was difficult for me, wondering if Mark forgot that God loved him each time I walked out the door.

Once Gail came with me for a visit. It had been a couple of weeks since I'd seen Mark. Now, as we walked into his room, we had to reintroduce ourselves.

"Hi, Mark," I said. "Remember me?"

He looked at me with a searching expression, as if to say, "No, never seen you before."

As I unpacked my guitar, I explained who we were. "Remember now, Mark?" Still no response.

I decided to start with his favorite, "Praise the Name of Jesus." He moved right along with the song, just as he always did. When we finished, I asked if he remembered singing it with me before. I had made sure to sing it every time I came.

Mark still had a lost expression. He just shook his head.

Of course not, I told myself. Mark couldn't help his loss of memory, not in the least. But I still felt sad. I couldn't help wishing I had some way of knowing that something was sinking in.

At that point, Gail brought out her Bible.

"Mark, I've got something I want to read you," she said. She opened to Isaiah 53. "It's about Jesus, our Savior."

Gail explained it all—who Jesus was, why he came, and what he had done for us on the Cross. All along, Mark's eyes were wide open, gazing at Gail intensely. Every few minutes he would mutter, "Wow . . . wow . . ."

When Gail finished, I turned to Mark. "Would you like to pray, Mark?" I asked.

He nodded. I led him in prayer, asking Christ to fill him with his love. Mark nodded along the entire time.

As Gail and I left the hospital that day, we knew that something very definite, something very real, had happened with Mark.

"Let it stick, God," we prayed on the way home. "Let it stay in his heart this time, just this once."

Two weeks later, as Gail and I drove back to the hospital for another visit, we had our hopes up. This time Mark had been wheeled into another room. Now he shared a room with Mama Jane's son, Keith.

"Hi, guys," I said.

"Hi, Mark," Gail said. "Remember us?"

Mark gave us that familiar, faraway look. It was as if he were saying, "No—who are you?"

"That's okay, Mark," Gail said. "We're John and Gail. We've come to read the Bible with you and to worship the Lord."

Mark just stared. It was clear he was curious as to who these strangers in his room might be.

I brought out my guitar to begin worship.

"Let's start our time with a worship chorus, guys," I said. "We'll sing 'Praise the Name of Jesus.' You know that one, don't you, Mark?"

Mark continued to stare.

We began the chorus. Gail and I harmonized together, knowing that neither Keith nor Mark could sing along.

Then, suddenly, we heard a voice singing along with us. It was Mark's.

"Prai th name o Jesah . . ."

Gail and I glanced at each other in astonishment. The voice continued:

"Prai th name o Jesah . . . He mah rock. He mah fo-treh. He mah deverah, him I truh . . ."

Mark's face was intense, full of emotion. It was a look of deep joy.

Gail smiled at me.

Mark hadn't remembered us. But somewhere lodged away in his memory—in a place nobody knew, in a way nobody could explain—was the most important thing of all: the love of God, expressed through music.

Music. It's one of the languages of the voiceless.

Voicing the Questions:
The Path to Hope

8

Most of us are afraid of our own questions. This is true especially of people of faith. We're afraid that by raising questions, we're violating our faith. We think our questions drive us away from trust, from truth, from God himself.

The fact is, our questions don't drive us away from God. They drive us *to* him. I've never seen anybody who questioned or struggled genuinely with God not end up finding him.

Yet, for those of us who are in the work of ministry, questioning often feels like a taboo. I'm no exception. For years I never felt comfortable questioning God or faith. I was afraid of shaking my stability, of losing my spiritual moorings.

Then, John Samuel died. And that changed everything. Suddenly, I was the one broken and in need. I was the one asking the unanswerable questions. I was the parent standing by the hospital bed, wondering, "Why?"

And I can honestly tell you, I've learned more about God's love from asking that question—from being needy and broken—than from anything else. Being in that position has also taught me about doing the work of ministry in God's strength, not my own.

I remember a time when it was getting harder and harder to go by myself to the head-injury hospitals. Every time I went, I got depressed. It reminded me of how I felt whenever I picked up Gail from her job as a nurse's aid at a rest home during our dating days. I could never go inside to meet her; I had to wait for her in my car.

This probably came from my growing-up years. During certain periods of my childhood, members of my family and I were always visiting doctors and hospitals. It was always unsettling to me, never knowing if they were going to come out okay. It caused me to be nauseous. After that, whenever hospitals came into the picture, the same feeling came over me. And it never really left.

In fact, that's the irony in what I felt called to do. The old feeling plagued me the first time I walked into a head-trauma center. I had to fight it just to do what I did with head-injury patients. Over time, I'd fought off the nausea with a fair amount of success. But now, going by myself to the hospitals, the old feeling had started to come back.

Finally, I admitted to Gail, "I don't think I can go by myself anymore. It's gotten too hard. I feel like I don't have anything to give anybody."

Yet, as I drove to Milford one day, feeling that awful feeling, I was sure of only one thing. I simply had to go on.

When I walked into the hospital, a caseworker came up to me. "Hey, John," she waved. "Have you met Trudy O'Shea yet?"

I didn't recognize the name. "No, I haven't."

"Well, she's out on the porch with her husband, Ron. He's in a wheelchair. Why don't you go out and introduce yourself?"

That was the last thing I wanted to do. *Hello, I'm John, and I feel like crap today. How are you?* I always hated having to explain what I do, especially to strangers. I was afraid of how crazy it sounded to most people.

But I knew I had to go.

When I walked onto the porch, I saw a woman standing behind a man in a wheelchair. There was another couple standing beside them. "Excuse me," I asked, "is one of you Trudy O'Shea?"

"Yes, that's me," said the woman behind the wheelchair. Sitting in it was obviously Ron, her husband. He was silent, clearly comatose at some level.

I explained who I was and told them what I did. I was self-conscious the whole time, especially with the other couple standing there. I kept it short and to the point. It was the best I could offer under the circumstances.

When I finished, the man standing nearby whispered, "Praise the Lord."

It caught me off guard. "I'm sorry," I said. "What did you say?"

"Praise the Lord!" he said, this time a little louder. Then the man began to cry.

The woman next to him—evidently, his wife—patted his shoulder. Then she reached down and patted the man in the wheelchair.

"This is my brother, Ron," she said. At that point, she began to cry, too.

The weeping man told me, "I'm Freddie. And this is my wife, Cindy. I'm a pastor in Missouri. We've been praying for over a year that God would send someone here to minister to my brother-in-law."

Suddenly, I felt like shrinking into the woodwork. Here this pastor was thanking the Lord for me, God's "man of the hour." He had no idea how I'd been feeling. Just a little while before, I was seriously wondering whether I'd ever be able to go into a hospital again.

Freddie was beaming. "Our truck broke down. We were supposed to leave three days ago, but we couldn't. I guess we were supposed to be here to meet you."

They cried and hugged each other.

These people were real. In fact, their vulnerability was so touching, I couldn't hold back. I opened up to them about what I'd been experiencing.

"Before you make me out to be some kind of hero," I said, "you've got to know that just a few hours ago, I wasn't coming here at all. I'm—well, I'm just glad I'm here now."

We talked and encouraged one another for a while. It was a wonderful time. I learned in that time that the injured man, Ron O'Shea, was a mid-level patient. He coughed and hacked the whole time we talked. He wasn't a Christian and neither was Trudy.

I asked Freddie and Cindy when they planned to leave.

"Well, the truck's fixed now," Freddie said. "We've got to get back home as soon as we can."

"Can you stay till tomorrow?" I asked.

"Yes. I suppose we could leave sometime toward evening."

"Good," I said. "I'd like to set up a time when we could meet here tomorrow to have a time of worship with Ron."

I arranged it all with the volunteer director. When I came back the next day, the two couples were waiting for me in a conference room. Ron O'Shea was hacking and coughing terribly. He looked miserable.

"Ron," I told him, "I'm going to play my guitar. And we're all going to worship together and pray for you. You can join us if you want to."

I turned to Trudy. "Do you mind if I pray for your husband's healing?"

She looked a little spooked. Freddie and Cindy were a bit sheepish. But they agreed.

"Father," I prayed, "please touch Ron's body. Do this however you choose to. But touch his heart as well. Let him know your love. I pray that today he knows you in a way he never has before."

With that, I began singing a chorus. The others gradually joined me, and we went from one chorus to another, singing for a good forty-five minutes.

During that time, Ron never coughed once. He looked totally at peace. Toward the end, a tear streamed out of his eye. Then, more tears came. His family had never seen him do that before.

Trudy turned to me, crying. "John, thank you," she said. "I know this is just what he needs."

Then she began weeping openly. "I don't know what to say," she finally said to me. "But . . . but I want to believe like you do."

Freddie and Cindy smiled.

Trudy called her daughter into the room. "Honey, John is going to pray for us."

We all prayed for Trudy and her daughter. Their beaming faces were evidence of what they both felt. I could only guess that Ron experienced something too. By the time we ended, the family was hugging and crying.

"I'm glad we were here to meet you yesterday," Freddie said, clutching my hand. "God knew we needed to meet you.

I agreed. "He knew we all needed something."

I lost contact with the O'Sheas, because soon afterward John was moved to another facility. But I did stay in touch with Freddie and Cindy. They even came to New York several times. As I thought about it, I couldn't believe how I had nearly missed the chance to meet these wonderful people. And it all happened in spite of my weakness. When I was at my lowest point, God carried me.

He carried us all.

In every hospital where I sing, I meet people who tell me they've been praying for someone to come visit a loved one— someone to bring life and hope to them.

Ron O'Shea may still be in a wheelchair somewhere. He may not have received the "answers" we all hope for: physical healing, wholeness of body and mind. But the fact is, we all tasted something of God's healing that day.

Our questions lead us to *him*. And an encounter with him always brings hope.

Mike Labarca was a teenager in a high-level coma in the same hospital where I met the O'Sheas. When I met Mike's father, he seemed friendly but a little distant. Mike's mother, Vicki, however, was another story. Her face was an open book. And it had the familiar look of a parent whose child has suffered a coma. It's a mixture of bewilderment and desperation.

Yet Vicki seemed different. Whereas most parents of comatose kids were shocked and directionless, Vicki seemed on an active hunt for God. In fact, the week before, she had asked me to pray with her.

Now, as I signed in, I was hopeful for the Labarca family. I was looking forward to seeing them that day. But my first order of business was to visit an eighteen-year-old girl named Christina. Vicki Labarca had told me about her. I hadn't met Christina's mother yet, but Vicki had already told her about me. Vicki had made sure I'd gotten permission from the mother to see Christina.

I scanned the list at the front desk for Christina's room number. When I found it, I made my way down the hallway to her room, and as I turned the corner, I saw the Labarcas down at the other end of the corridor. The moment they saw me, they smiled.

"Hi, John!" Vicki shouted from the end of the hall. Both she and her husband looked much better than they had the week before. Mr. Labarca especially seemed different. He was smiling as broadly as Vicki. As they came nearer, both their faces lit up like lightbulbs.

"How are you doing?" I asked.

"Wonderful!" Vicki blurted. "We were hoping you'd come again to see Mike."

They filled me in briefly on their son's condition. Mostly, however, they just beamed. Something definitely had happened since last week.

"We'll be here all day," Vicki said, "so whenever you want to come see Mike is fine."

"Good,"I said. "I want to fit in some other people, including Christina."

As we parted, I shook my head in wonder. What a difference a week had made.

I walked down the hall toward Christina's room, wondering what her condition might be. Vicki had never mentioned it. As I tiptoed in, I saw a girl lying in bed, seemingly lifeless. She was just like many other young patients I'd seen and worked with.

Near the bed were pictures of a young girl dressed in a cap and gown for her high-school graduation. I looked at the form in the bed; she looked nothing like the vibrant image of life in the picture. Christina's body had contorted from her brain's betrayal of her muscles and nerves. I'd still never gotten used to seeing a person's coma-ravaged body for the first time.

I pulled up a chair from the corner and sat down next to the bed. As I unpacked my guitar, I introduced myself to Christina. I spoke to her for a while, assuring her of God's love. I told her he had the ability to touch her deep inside, where no one else could. Then I started singing.

It ended up being one of those times I just didn't want to stop. I sang and prayed next to Christina for nearly an hour.

But I easily could have continued all day long. I was being energized, just as I sensed Christina was being touched.

Finally, as I stood to leave, I turned and caught a glimpse of a woman standing at the door. Apparently, she'd been there for some time.

"Hello," she said, "I'm Christina's mother. I heard you singing, and I didn't want to interrupt."

"It's good to meet you," I said. "But you need to know something. Anytime you're here, you're welcome to come in too. You need to be encouraged just as much as she does."

The woman's eyes welled with tears. They revealed what was in her heart: She needed to talk.

"Would you like to go with me to the lounge?" I asked. "Maybe we could spend a few minutes talking."

She looked relieved. We walked to the end of the hall and sat at a table near the snack bar. As soon as we sat down, she began pouring her heart out to me. This thing with her daughter, she said—the accident, the coma, the "not knowing" from day to day—she'd really been going through it. Yet she couldn't voice the question that sat poised on the edge of her heart: *Why?*

I asked how her husband was handling everything. She simply started crying. For several minutes the tears just kept coming.

In the corner of my eye, I noticed another woman sitting nearby. She was trying to hear our conversation. I was certain she could hear every word.

Christina's mother just kept crying.

"Listen," I said, "we all question God at times." I paused. "There is one thing I can do. I can pray for you. And I believe God will give you strength. Would you let me pray with you?"

She nodded.

I looked toward the other woman. Her eyes were hungry, almost pleading.

"Why don't you come over and sit with us?" I offered.

She quietly pulled up a chair and sat down. She reached out and patted Christina's mother's arm.

Now I remembered seeing this woman before. I'd caught sight of her wheeling a young man—apparently her son— around the halls by herself.

I prayed for both women. Each one let out a flood of tears. When I finished, I glanced up. Christina's mother was still weeping, but she smiled.

"Thank you," she said again and again. "Thank you."

We all just sat there for a long time.

Time had flown. It was getting late now, and I wanted to spend time with Mike Labarca and his parents. I picked up my guitar and started through the lounge doors.

Yet, as I turned just outside the room, something told me to go back. There was something about that second woman— the one who'd sat at the table with us.

I walked back in, pulled a chair from the table, and sat down across from her. Her flood of tears started again. She just began pouring everything out.

"I don't understand what's wrong with this world," she choked in a thick Brooklyn accent. "There's hatred, evil. The Jews are killing blacks, the blacks are killing Jews. When I look around at everything, I have such little faith. I look at my son"—at this point, her shoulders began to heave with sobs—"and I don't have much faith."

"I can understand that," I said. "I struggle with that too. We see the darkness and the brokenness all around us, and it starts to rob us of our faith. God's the only one who really understands what's in our hearts."

She didn't seem to know what to say. She reached up and squeezed my hand. "Just keep doing what you're doing," she cried softly. "We need people like you."

"I'll stop in and see you next time," I promised. "We'll talk again."

She nodded. "I'd like that."

I picked up my guitar once again and started out the lounge door and down the hall. Suddenly, her words struck home in my heart. I realized, *If you just go and sit with these people, it's enough. God can work through that.*

Suddenly, I realized: *That's the point.*

You don't even need to be strong yourself. He works through your caring and listening.

In five minutes' time, two utterly broken human beings had experienced a taste of a different kind of love. That love had entered their worst tragedies in a way nothing else could. Vicki Labarca, desperate herself just the week before, had pointed me to Christina's mother. And Christina's mother, without knowing it, had drawn in another hurting mother. In the space of a week—and a brief, few minutes today in the hospital lounge—all three had encountered God. He had invited their questions. And their voices had been heard.

I thought of the Labarcas and our prayer the week before. I'd already seen love at work in them. It was all over their faces now.

I couldn't wait to get to Mike's room.

When I walked in, Vicki Labarca was leaning over her son's bed. She was speaking to him as she would to anyone else. "Mike, you can trust God," she was saying. "You can believe him to work out everything for good."

I could hardly believe what I was hearing.

Vicki and her husband turned and saw me. "Hi, John," they both said, beckoning me in. I sat down next to them.

They told me how Mike was doing. Only this time, they were completely different people from the week before. After a few minutes, Vicki leaned back in her chair and looked at me with an expression of wonder.

"John, I'm so close to God now," she said. "I used to think I was, but I wasn't."

I smiled. Inside, I was doing cartwheels.

"That Scripture you just quoted to Mike," I said, "that's something God wants to show us firsthand. None of us knows what he's got in mind for us. But we can believe he's eventually going to work all things for our good. Even if it's in heaven when we see it."

I turned to Mike, who lay motionless. Above him, taped to the walls and standing on a shelf, were pictures of him in a football uniform. He had been a standout player.

"Mike, we've only seen each other a couple of times," I began, "but I want you to know something about me."

I wasn't sure how either Vicki or her husband would take this—but I told Mike my story. I told him how I had attended college in Ohio on a football scholarship, how a knee injury had ended every dream I'd had, and how devastating it all had been.

"It wasn't until my life came to an end, along with all the plans I'd made, that God got control of my life," I said. Then I gave him the good news about God's love for him.

Vicki had been staring at me the whole time. I couldn't tell if I'd burst their bubble and dashed their hopes about their son, or if somehow they could see the meaning in what I'd told him.

"I didn't know anything about you," Vicki said. "I'm so glad you shared that with us."

Mr. Labarca was listening intently to every word. I nodded toward Mike.

"Even if nothing changes in his circumstances," I said, "God still loves him—and us. That's what we have to hold on to."

Before I knew it, it was almost two o'clock. I had been talking with the Labarcas for over an hour. Gail would have dinner ready in a couple of hours; I had to start for home.

As I left the Labarcas in the room with Mike, I turned to get one last glimpse of their smiling faces. I thought, *It would be hard for anybody looking into this room not to know what that expression is.*

It was hope.

I didn't know what life had in store for Mike Labarca. But as I walked down the front steps of the hospital, one word kept emerging from my heart and forming a lump in my throat: *hope.*

The road home seemed to stretch out forever. I passed all the old road signs, all the hills, the country stores, and roadside diners, the curves in the road I knew by heart. They all looked new to me today.

As I drove along, thinking about all that God had done in a single day, I remembered the words I'd heard from a speaker at a men's retreat just a couple of weeks before.

"Hope," the man had said, "is something that is absolutely certain because God has promised it. It just hasn't happened yet."

So much like faith: *The substance of things hoped for. The evidence of things not seen.*

That is the kind of hope—true, alive, and lasting forever—that I'd seen that day. Jesus had reached deep into those hurting people's hearts—and mine—and had revealed the truth about himself: He absolutely loves us. *Absolutely.* And his all-encompassing, absolute love becomes all the more clear when we're facing life's hardest questions.

That hope stays with me today. It helps me remember that God invites all my unspoken questions. All my doubting and struggling and despairing over my dead son. And he hears all the voiceless cries of my heart, even when I don't know they're there. He loves me, no matter what.

No matter what.

That's what has sustained me, ever since I began this work: hope. It has kept me around these hospitals, despite my weakness and discouragement, to see things I never would have seen otherwise. Things I was blind to, but that happened every day. I've seen the love of God bring light even to the darkness of an irreversible coma.

We are all in darkness, at one time or another. Most of us have known, at various points in our lives, what it's like to be weak, needy, helpless, voiceless. And the Bible tells us we can experience the strength of God *in that very weakness.* That is, if we don't fight it—and instead, allow it to turn us toward the face of God.

When we question, we *need* God.

And without the questions, there is no need.

I've learned that, like the Scripture says, when we're faithless, he still remains faithful. Because it's all about his faithfulness to us. Our job is what the real work of ministry is all about: *needing him.*

Blessed are the poor in spirit—those whose hearts ache with need—for truly, they shall see God.

An Invitation
from the Voiceless

So, who are the voiceless? And what do they have to say to us?

Think of some of the people you've just read about:

A man who once could not speak, but who now says he became a Christian while in a coma.

A death-row prisoner who's no longer on earth, but whose life continues to demonstrate the joy of giving our all, every day.

Two young women in the eye of a media storm, who beg just to be seen for the human beings they are.

A small group of regular guys, trying to endure the daily rigors of life with severe head injuries.

My son, who lived his short life listening to the songs of heaven.

What do the voiceless have to say?

They remind us of questions. Questions we all have—deep questions, important questions about life and faith and health and heaven. Questions that, if they hadn't been raised by the voiceless among us, might have remained locked away forever in our hearts.

The voiceless free us to ask questions of God himself, a God who tells us we can come at any time and reason together with him (Isaiah 1:18). A God who encourages us to voice our questions to him, as Job did, because he doesn't flinch from any of them.

The voiceless remind us that God invites us to live not by rules alone but by a love that sees a need—a love that's not afraid to give what appears impractical (John 12:3–8).

They encourage us not to expect a tidy life but instead to believe in a God who's much larger than we ever imagined him to be (Ephesians 3:20).

They tell us to seek God not in some sweet, neat package of answers but to look for him in a world that's messy, full of problems, and crying out to be redeemed (Romans 8:22).

The voiceless remind us that when there are no longer any words—no airtight theology, no carefully designed plans of action—that there is always music (the book of Psalms).

We may know the words. But sometimes we don't know the music.

The voiceless do.

They sing to us the songs of heaven, reminding us we can see eternity in the present—right now, today, in the midst of our everyday, ordinary lives.

If you would like more information on John and Gail Wessells' work, write to:

Precious Oil Ministries
P.O. Box 511
Otego, New York 13825
email: PreciousJW@aol.com.

Also, if you'd like information on John Wessells' CD, *Tell Him for Me* or other related music, visit him on the web @ www.preciousoilministries.com.

We want to hear from you. Please send your comments about this book to us in care of zreview@zondervan.com. Thank you.

GRAND RAPIDS, MICHIGAN 49530 USA

WWW.ZONDERVAN.COM